ENGLISH HUMOUR

by

J. B. PRIESTLEY

" Here was a merry world, my masters ! "

LONGMANS, GREEN AND CO.
LONDON ⬧ NEW YORK ⬧ TORONTO
1929

Made in Great Britain

INTRODUCTION

I HAVE been asked to write an introduction to a series of volumes to be published under the general title of "*The English Heritage.*" I think the editors and the publishers are to be warmly congratulated on their enterprise, and I find a peculiar pleasure in contributing a few words of welcome in a preface in which I may use the word English without fear of interruption, and speak of England without hearing the acidulated suggestion that I should say Britain.

These books are the more needed because much of what they treat is changing under our eyes, and it may be of interest to our children to look to the rock whence they are hewed; and to others it may be a revealing of the Englishman and of his heritage, for he is not apt to speak before strangers either of his land or of himself, and when he does the less Englishman he.

The choice of subject appears to me to be singularly happy. Think, for a moment, of the centuries packed into a little volume on "The County Spirit." That spirit, tranquil, unperceived, and apparently forgotten in our cities, leaped in a moment into a flame which swept across the battlefields of the world. Quickened, revivified, it is in our bones, as it has been since our counties were carved out of the dissipating fragments of the Heptarchy.

Last Whitsuntide I was a pilgrim among our graveyards in Flanders and on the Somme. In one of the most beautiful, where all are beautiful, I met three other pilgrims, large silent men. Two carried baskets, and one was rapidly scanning each head-stone and occasionally stooped to the ground. I approached them, and we spoke together. They had brought out from home a quantity of small white-enamelled tablets with spikes affixed, the device thereon a red rose and the legend, "They win or die who wear the Red Rose of Lancaster," and the stooping man had been placing one at the headstone of every grave which held a Lancastrian soldier. So might their ancestors have murmured the same words over the bloody fields of Barnet and of Tewkesbury.

Happy, too, is he who writes of "The Parish Church." In variety, in beauty of architecture and of situation, they are incomparable. But the parish itself has become a unit so small as to be almost unnoticed in these days of rapid locomotion. Nothing is harder for the post-motor generation to realize than that in an age of horse-drawn vehicles you lived at the centre of a circle with a six-mile radius, or on special occasions one of twice that length. It was impossible for people to go away for week-ends or to visit friends in the next county on a Sunday. The parish church which only opened on Sunday in the days of my childhood became, in fact, the meeting-place of the neighbour-hood on that day, and I can see once again the pony cart and the landau on the road, people in knots of two or three coming down the lanes, and the little crowd that gathered in the churchyard, discussing the events of the past week, while the peal of bells, whose music had been the companion of the last half-hour of our walk, yielded to the urgent shriller note of the five minutes' bell. Then the smell of freshly-baked loaves in the porch, waiting for distribution after the service, the baize door, and we passed into the church to the big pew in which I spent so much time counting the ten torteaux in pile of the Episcopal arms in the east window, and trying to catch the wandering eye of one of our servants in the gallery. Most of the men in the congregation came in tall hats, and the older labourers still wore their smocks.

More than fifty years have passed, and this picture of a vanished England comes before my eyes more vividly each year I live.

But no less happy is the task of him who writes of "The English Road," and it is well that our children should know something of those roads their fathers tramped and loved as did their fathers before them for forty generations. Fifty years hence may be published an up-to-date series of such books as we now offer under the title, "Our Heritage and what we made of it."

I could show you many a ten or twenty miles of road in England where every turn opens out a fresh picture to make you draw in your breath with sheer delight, where the roadside timber is yet undisturbed, and where the black-and-white cottage at the bend, with its garden scented with gilly-flowers, makes such an awkward corner for the motorist; and here and there the little inn, even as it was when Glutton met Peronel of Flanders in the days when Langland lay on the slopes of Malvern Hill. And even now when the cider is growing warm in china mugs on the hob in the inner parlour, some bowman on his long journey home from Agincourt or some pikeman from Naseby would find there the same kindly company, the same broad speech, the same wise, tolerant native humour of that world in which he was born.

But I dare not linger in the alehouse; this is a preface, and a preface is like the speech of a chairman introducing a speaker—it cannot be too brief.

How often we find the smithy just outside, and that is as it should be, for the smith's is thirsty work. I had many ambitions as a child; one was to be a blacksmith. What more exciting than the roar of the blast, a. even now I can still feel the thrill which stirred my small heart when I was allowed to work the big bellow. I remember riding down the lane to get my pony shod, and the very spot where I could first hear the ringing of the hammers. How exciting, too, the smell of the smithy! The curious acrid smell of water thrown on the red-hot iron, the warm steam of the cart-horses, the burning hoof when the shoe was being fitted. And how I admired when the smith himself hit the shoe by accident against his palm and nothing happened but the sizzling noise of burnt horn and an exclamation of justifiable dissatisfaction at his own clumsy workmanship. How I longed to have a horny hand!

As these memories crowd back upon me I cannot

help thinking of the happiness which these books will bring to countless readers, and I am permitted to envy those who are so fortunate as to write for this series no less than those who will read what they have written.

STANLEY BALDWIN.

CONTENTS

CHAP.   PAGE

INTRODUCTION V

I. THE ENGLISH CHARACTER . . . I

II. CLOWNS AND COMEDIANS . . . 22

III. COMIC ART 46

IV. A GALLOP AND A GOSSIP—I . . . 62

V. A GALLOP AND A GOSSIP—II . . 84

VI. THREE NOVELISTS 119

VII. CHARLES LAMB 138

VIII. DICKENS 150

IX. SHAKESPEARE 163

ENGLISH HUMOUR

CHAPTER I

THE ENGLISH CHARACTER

IT is curious that so few foreigners have noticed that we English are a humorous race. If we consult travellers' tales we shall discover that they are anything but consistent: now they say we are an industrious people, now a lazy; sometimes we are described as being cruel and arrogant, at other times as being unusually kind and good-humoured. There is, however, some measure of agreement among all these visitors. We do not find them saying that the chief defects of the English character are timidity and an absence of self-confidence and self-approval. Most of them would agree with that seventeenth-century Italian visitor who said: "They are of a most manly spirit, and valiant even to rashness in war both by land and sea"; or with the Venetian Ambassador who remarked: "The English are great lovers of themselves and of everything belonging to them. They think there are no other men like themselves, and no other world but England; and whenever they see a handsome foreigner, they say that he looks like an Englishman, and that it is a great pity he should not be an Englishman; and when they set any delicacy before a foreigner they ask him if such a thing is made in his country." It is generally agreed, too, that we are very fond of good living: "They woneth to gluttony more than other men, and are more costly in meat and drink and clothing"; and again: "The whole nation, beyond all other mortal men, is most given to banqueting and feasts"; and this—a shrewd French thrust— "The English may be easily brought to anything, provided you fill their bellies, let them have freedom of speech, and do not bear too hard upon their lazy temper." We catch a glimpse here of an idle junketing race, of that Merry England in which we have always believed in our heart of hearts, however grim the actual records may be. Yet we have bestowed the title ourselves; these foreigners do not mention a Merry England. On the contrary, the greater number of them declare roundly that we are a melancholy and saturnine and morose people.

The legend goes back so far that it may be found embodied in a mediæval Latin proverb: *Anglica gens est optima flens et pessima ridens*; an astonishing verdict, for whatever our capacity for laughter may be, or may have been, we cannot imagine that at any time the English wept more easily and copiously than other races. Whether Froissart said or did not say that we amused ourselves sadly after the fashion of our country (and the actual remark is found first in the Duc de Sully's *Memoirs*, where it runs, *Les Anglais s'amusent tristement selon l'usage de leur pays*), the fact remains that a great many of his countrymen have repeated it, or made variations upon it, every time it has been necessary to describe us. The legend of our melancholy and moroseness has persisted for centuries in France. One visitor she sent us in the

eighteenth century returned to tell his readers that
the authorities in London took care to block up the
approaches to the Thames in order that a glimpse of
the river should not tempt their citizens to suicide.
Yet these precautions, he observes blandly, were
without effect, so determined were the English, lost
in their native gloom, to put an end to their lives.
The legend can show us nothing better than that.
When Emerson began his account of our character,
in his *English Traits*, he remarked upon this
tradition:

> The English race are reputed morose. I do
> not know that they have sadder brows than their
> neighbours of northern climates. They are sad
> by comparison with the singing and dancing
> nations: not sadder, but slow and staid, as finding
> their joys at home. They, too, believe that where
> there is no enjoyment of life, there can be no
> vigour and art in speech or thought; that your
> merry heart goes all the way, your sad heart tires
> in a mile. This trait of gloom has been fixed on
> them by French travellers, who, from Froissart,
> Voltaire, Le Sage, Mirabeau, down to the lively
> journalists of the *feuilletons*, have spent their wit
> on the solemnity of their neighbours. The French
> say, gay conversation is unknown in their island:
> the Englishman finds no relief from reflection
> except in reflection: when he wishes for amuse-
> ment, he goes to work: his hilarity is like an
> attack of fever. Religion, the theatre, and the
> reading the books of his country, all feed and
> increase his natural melancholy. The police does

not interfere with public diversions. It thinks itself bound in duty to respect the pleasures and rare gaiety of this inconsolable nation; and their well-known courage is entirely attributable to their disgust for life. . . .

We can find many excuses, however, for those foreign visitors, and especially the Frenchmen, who have come so quickly to the conclusion that we are for ever morose and melancholy. England is the land of privacy, and, therefore, the stranger who comes here is at a disadvantage. He sees the high walls, but not the gardens they enclose. He watches Englishmen hurrying silently through the streets to their homes, and does not realize that they are hastening away, out of his sight, only in order that they may unbend at last, turning themselves into persons he would not recognize. He hears us whispering together in public places and concludes that we are exchanging trade figures or doleful news, and not little jokes that he would not understand even if he heard them. A French visitor, finding none of that public gaiety which he has come to associate with a pleasurable life, at once imagines that here is nothing but gloom, a whole nation fog-bound in its wits. He forgets, if he ever knew, that nearly everything in England that is of any importance is private and personal, that even our jokes have walls and hedges round them, that there may be a great deal of laughter here that escapes his ears. He will readily fall into the error of imagining that London is a sad city, just as the travelling Englishman comes too easily to the conclusion that Paris is a very gay city.

It is likely that both of them have been misled by surface appearances. We can forgive our French visitor, however, once we realize that he is looking for something he cannot find on this side of the Channel. Life in France is leavened by wit, and life in England is leavened by humour. But French wit has about it a public air, has a background of highly-organized social life; you can see it flashing down the crowded boulevards; and even the visitor who is ignorant of the language is aware of its presence as he watches the vivacious groups round the little tables. English humour, on the other hand, is curiously private and domestic, offering nothing to the casual arrival from other countries; it is part of the atmosphere of the place, a hazy light on things; it manifests itself in innumerable slow grins and chuckles; it is not something that can be picked up with the language, but something that must be given time to filter through; and thus, while it is everywhere, a traveller in a hurry might well be excused for not noticing that it is here at all.

It is from those rare travellers who are not in a hurry, who remain with us and brood over us and yet take care, however long their stay, not to be engulfed in our life, to remain detached, that we learn most about ourselves. Such a one is Mr. George Santayana, who has repaid a hundredfold whatever hospitality this island may have offered him by his *Soliloquies in England*. In this volume of wise and exquisitely embroidered meditations, he does not discuss the subject of English humour, but he does what is, for our purpose here, the next best thing, he discusses the English character with acuteness and unusual sympathy. He asks what it is that governs the Englishman. After replying that it is certainly not intelligence, nor seldom passion, and hardly self-interest, he goes on:

the Englishman

read + end here

> If we tried to say that what governs him is convention, we should have to ask ourselves how it comes about that England is the paradise of individuality, eccentricity, heresy, anomalies, hobbies, and humours. Nowhere do we come oftener upon those two social abortions—the affected and the disaffected. Where else would a man inform you, with a sort of proud challenge, that he lived on nuts, or was in correspondence through a medium with Sir Joshua Reynolds, or had been disgustingly housed when last in prison?

Here we may break in to point out that these things of which "England is the paradise" are excellent subject-matter for the humorist, who asks nothing better than to be surrounded by people who are strongly individualistic or eccentric, delighting in heresies, crammed with humours, and all mounted on hobby-horses. We can echo that cry of Mr. Squeers when he tastes the milk and water: "Here's richness!" But Mr. Santayana is waiting to answer his question:

> Let me come to the point boldly; what governs the Englishman is his inner atmosphere, the weather in his soul. It is nothing particularly spiritual or mysterious. When he has taken his exercise and is drinking his tea or his beer and

lighting his pipe; when, in his garden or by his fire, he sprawls in an aggressively comfortable chair; when, well-washed and well-brushed, he resolutely turns in church to the east and recites the Creed (with genuflexions, if he likes genu-flexions) without in the least implying that he believes one word of it; when he hears or sings the most crudely sentimental and thinnest of popular songs, unmoved but not disgusted; when he makes up his mind who is his best friend or his favourite poet; when he adopts a party or a sweet-heart; when he is hunting or shooting or boating, or striding through the fields; when he is choosing his clothes or his profession—never is it a precise reason, or purpose, or outer fact that determines him; it is always the atmosphere of his inner man.

To say that this atmosphere was simply a sense of physical well-being, of coursing blood and a prosperous digestion, would be far too gross; for while psychic weather is all that, it is also a witness to some settled disposition, some ripening inclina-tion for this or that, deeply rooted in the soul. It gives a sense of direction in life which is virtually a code of ethics, and a religion behind religion. On the other hand, to say it was the vision of any ideal or allegiance to any principle would be making it far too articulate and abstract. The inner atmosphere, when compelled to condense into words, may precipitate some curt maxim or over-simple theory as a sort of war cry; but its puerile language does it injustice, because it broods at a much deeper level than language or even thought. It is a mass of dumb instinct and allegiances, the love of a certain quality of life, to be maintained manfully.

We might say that this inner atmosphere, this weather in the soul, is just as much the secret of English humour as the outer atmosphere, the real weather, is the secret of our delectable English landscapes. Our fields and woods and hills are more often than not covered with mists so light that they are nothing but a haze, in which hard edges are rubbed away and colours are softened and blended; the fields will suddenly be silvered, the woods will be full of a golden smoke, the hills will take on the bloom of ripe damsons, and the sky will be a wash of delicate colouring as if some water-colourist were for ever at work there; and this is the sensitive, the misty-eyed and faintly flushing face of England that is at once the despair and the delight of her artists. The English mind is like this landscape of hers. There, too, is a haze, rubbing away the hard edges of ideas, softening and blending the hues of passion. Reason is there but it is not all-conquering and triumphant, setting up its pyramids and obelisks or marking out long straight roads down which the battalions of thought must march. The country does not show a face like a glaring map; nothing is clearly marked out, and no boundaries can be discovered; the solid earth is there but sunlight and mist have given it a vague enchantment. Let the sunlight disappear, and everything is grey and very soon seems heavy and sodden. Let the mist be completely banished and the land lie naked and quivering in the sunlight, and there is an end to this enchantment. This, then, is the English mind, where mirth and melancholy play like light and shadow, sunshine and mist; a mind that, once robbed of its bloom and golden haze, is utterly without charm, giving us the leaden-eyed Englishman of the satirists. Fortunately that bloom and that golden haze are there for ever in the long splendour of English literature.

There is something that we may call English humour. We may call it that not merely because England must have her own share of the ludicrous just as she has of the birds or the flowers, the wind and the rain, not merely because there is laughter in London as well as laughter in Paris or Vienna; but because there is a humour that is not quite like any other, that has, at least, a twist in it that is purely English, a fact that we notice at once as soon as we have left the common ground of the laughing and the laughable, the universal guffaw. The drolleries of Shakespeare and Dickens, Lamb's Letters and *Alice in Wonderland*, did not make their appearance here by a happy accident: they are as English as the silvery fields that Constable painted. So native, indeed, is this humour of ours that many foreigners, as we have seen, commenting on the moving picture of our daily life and not on the set scene of our literature, have not even remarked its existence. It has not occured to them that we are a humorous race, that though we may not have gaiety, passion or logic, we have humour. It is as if we were so strange to these visitors that they could not tell whether we were laughing or crying, just as a traveller in an Eastern country might not know whether the music he heard was that of a funeral or a wedding. / How ironical it is that the country whose literature can show most laughter should be accused so frequently of not knowing what it is to laugh! Nor is there any escape by assuming what nobody has the right to assume, namely, that that literature does not mirror the real national temper. The innumerable humorists it can show us, like the lyrical poets, are not change-lings, they are Englishmen who have more vivacity of thought and greater powers of expression than their neighbours but whose minds work in the same way; and it is significant that the humorists proper—as distinct from the wits, the satirists, the ironists—have never had the least difficulty here in capturing the popular suffrages. We have seen how easily the foreign visitor may be misled; and his very inability to recognize those humorous traits in our character, his belief that our mirth and melancholy are one, really begins to define our humour. We have also seen what a detached and alien observer, disinterested and very wise, has made of the English mind. If we go a little further with him and try to approach English humour by way of his account of our national character, we shall at least be free from the charge of making no attempt to look at ourselves from the outside.

Here, then, is a companion passage by Mr. Santayana:

The secret of English mastery is self-mastery. The Englishman establishes a sort of satisfaction and equilibrium in his inner man, and from that citadel of rightness he easily measures the value of everything that comes within his moral horizon. In what may lie beyond he takes but a feeble interest. Enterprising enough when in a roving mood, and fond of collecting outlandish objects and ideas, he seldom allows his wanderings and discoveries to unhinge his home loyalties or ruffle his self-possession; and he remains, after all his adventures, intellectually as indolent and secure as in the beginning. As to speculative truth, he instinctively halts short of it, as it looms in the distance and threatens to cast a contemptuous and chilling shadow across his life. . . .

It we put this alongside the other passage, which describes "the inner atmosphere, the weather in the soul," we find that together they make up an account of the English character that will help us considerably to explain why we are, among other things, a race of humorists. Because we are individualists, living always for the inner man, we do not combine to bring things to one sharp test; yet because this "inner atmosphere," this "mass of dumb instincts and allegiances," is roughly the same for most of us, we can appeal to one another, offering judgments, with a fair measure of success. Thus we have standards, but not standards that are exactly known and acknowledged. Where all is known and acknowledged, one set of ideas ruling every mind, there may be wit in plenty—you may see it working like the guillotine—but there will be little humour. The mind must be free to play to be humorous. The doctrinaire, just because his mind is so completely made up and he has standards that he can apply instantly, may enjoy considerable power of wit and satire but he has no humour, and such laughter as he has will be savage and fully condemnatory. The Englishman rarely turns doctrinaire if only because he will not abandon himself to a few leading ideas and first principles, will not turn over that inner man, with his instincts and allegiances, to the drill sergeant of the intellect. It happens, however, that there are some features of English life that show us standards known and acknowledged—for example, social conduct in a certain class—and, as soon as these sides of life are approached, we are likely to get something lower than humour, laughter that is hard and condemnatory and not reflective and indulgent. It is as difficult for the snob to be a humorist as it is for the doctrinaire. On the other hand, had we no standards at all, if there was no inner atmosphere, no love of "a certain quality of life," nothing to which we could appeal in one another, humour would be impossible, for we could never declare of anything that it was really absurd. There are many good men and women in this predicament; they may laugh, but not a glimmer of humour ever visits the moonless prairie of their minds.

Again, because we are determined not by a precise reason, nor purpose, not outer fact—in Mr. Santa-yana's words—but by the atmosphere of the inner man, knowing more or less what we want and what we like but never knowing exactly why, it is perhaps easier for us English to achieve that balance of sympathy and antipathy necessary for the full appreciation of the ludicrous. Hazlitt saw this, though it is a pity that when he did see it he chanced

to be in one of his surliest moods and somewhat out
of temper with his countrymen :

The humour of English writing and description has often been wondered at; and it flows
from the same source as the merry traits of our
character. A degree of barbarism and rusticity
seems necessary to the perfection of humour.
The droll and laughable depend on peculiarity and
incongruity of character. But, with the progress
of refinement, the peculiarities of individuals and
of classes wear out or lose their sharp, abrupt
edges; nay, a certain slowness and dullness of
understanding is required to be struck with odd
and unaccountable appearances, for which a
greater facility of apprehension can sooner assign
an explanation that breaks the force of the seeming
absurdity, and to which a wide scope of imagination is more easily reconciled. Clowns and country
people are more amused, are more disposed to
laugh and make sport of the dress of strangers,
because from their ignorance the surprise is
greater, and they cannot conceive anything to be
natural or proper to which they are unused.
Without a given portion of hardness and repul-
siveness of feeling the ludicrous cannot well
exist. Wonder and curiosity, the attributes of inexperience, enter greatly into its composition.
Now it appears to me that the English are (or
were) just at that mean point between intelligence
and obtuseness, which must produce the most
abundant and happiest crop of humour. Absurdity
and singularity glide over the French mind without

jarring or jostling with it; or they evaporate in levity; with the Italians they are lost in indolence and pleasure. The ludicrous takes hold of the English imagination, and clings to it with all its ramifications. We resent any difference or peculiarity of appearance at first, and yet, having not much malice at our hearts, we are glad to turn it into a jest—we are liable to be offended, and as willing to be pleased—struck with oddity from not knowing what to make of it, we wonder and burst out a laughing at the eccentricity of others, while we follow our own bent from wilfulness or simplicity, and thus afford them, in our turn, matter for the indulgence of the comic vein. . . .

This is well said, but it shows some confusion of thought. Hazlitt is never quite sure whether he is discussing method or material, the marksman or the target. And while he is right in saying that wonder and curiosity are necessary for humour, he is obviously wrong in supposing that these are only "the attributes of inexperience." Wonder and curiosity may not necessarily indicate clownishness, for they happen to be present, too, wherever there is a powerful imagination. A Shakespeare can discover absurdities, can "be struck with odd and unaccountable appearances," like any rustic, but he could hardly be accused of having what Hazlitt says he ought to have: "a certain slowness and dullness of understanding." Yet, perhaps, in one sense, he could be so accused, for the very strength of his imagination, keeping alive that wonder and curiosity which are always active in children and simple people

and good poets, defeats that complacent understanding which turns us into men of the world and
shallow philosophers and cleverish persons. Such
an imagination would always keep its possessor
happily inexperienced, and would fill the world with
odd and unaccountable appearances. It is only fair
to Hazlitt, however, to say that we have taken him
away from his own ground, and are referring his
arguments to a different level of humour from that
he had in mind. But the latter part of his paragraph
is important, for there he notices that balance of
sympathy and antipathy which we have already
remarked in the English character. He sees that we
resent any difference or peculiarity but that we do not
resent it too much. Feeling tolerably sure of ourselves, we do not see in this difference or peculiarity
a very disturbing challenge; it does not anger or
frighten us; and so our slight resentment quickly
dissolves into laughter. This happens all the more
frequently because that intellectual indolence of ours
prevents us from inquiring gravely into the root
cause of any such difference or peculiarity. And
when these are merely a matter of appearance or
manners, which is what Hazlitt has in mind, the
laughter may be complacent and foolish itself, and
indeed often is. English humour is at its best and is
really most characteristic of the national mind when
it penetrates these surfaces and deals with character.

Here again, however, in the humour of character,
you may see the same attitude of mind at work.
There is a curious balance of sympathy and antipathy, but now the level has been raised; the little
resentment has become mockery, sharp as a needle

and quick as lightning, while the easy acquiescence, the tolerance, the good nature, on the other side are now affection and tenderness. Thus the humour of character might be described as tender mockery. It is to be found, of course, in some of the world's greatest literature, but it is also to be found, bubbling away, round the nearest corner, wherever there is a happy family. Husbands and wives, fathers and children, if they happen to be affectionate, fairly shrewd, and laughter-loving, appear to one another as comic characters in the best tradition of humour. The literature of this kind only universalizes a domestic joke. At one time it was thought that the humorist was completely antipathetic to his comic characters. Shakespeare was imagined shaking his head over the incorrigible Falstaff. Then it was observed that the great comic figures seemed to live in an atmosphere of affectionate indulgence, that the humorist delighted in his creatures and had not put them forward as bad examples or mere targets; and so critics concluded that sympathy and not antipathy was the secret of humour. You laughed, it was said, because you loved. But this view is clearly as false as the other. It is true that we laugh at those we love, but that is because we have come to know them so well, that certain traits or habits, as familiar to us as their faces, seem peculiarly absurd. These traits or habits are never those that we admire, and indeed we really resent them, but because they are joined with so much that is lovable, our resentment is checked by an opposing rush of tenderness and affection, and we find ourselves laughing. Thus these characteristics, so long as we are feeling indulgent, seem delightfully ridiculous; but when we happen to be out of patience, they may appear even detestable. It is essential that these traits or habits, which must be resented but not too actively resented, should be no great matter to us. It is likely that Smith's wife will not be amused by the fact that Smith occasionally gets drunk, whereas his friends may be highly amused and see him as a comic figure; but they, in their turn, will not see him long as a comic figure if he continually gets drunk, whereas people who merely heard stories about him or met him as a character in a book might roar with laughter at the fact that he was never sober. Again, neither in life nor literature (though we are, of course, far more tolerant in literature) do we find a really humorous character who flaunts the darkest and most terrible vices. In the East it might be possible to make a torturer or murderer into a comic figure, but it cannot be done here; our resentment would be so intense that it could not be dissolved into anything approaching honest and genial laughter. Even a Tartuffe is a figure of intellectual comedy and not of humour; and Pecksniff is only a humorous character now because we do not find our imagination really held by the action in which he takes part, because we enjoy him as a comic phrase-maker and do not believe in him as a villain. And Pecksniff is not one of our major comic characters. These are all at once odd and lovable, so constituted that though there are things about them that we cannot admire in a fellow creature and indeed might detest in someone else, our disapproval or contempt is counter-balanced by our affection for them, an affection that is only

B

increased by the entertainment they give us, for which we cannot help feeling grateful. By the time we have come to know the two parts of *Henry IV* we find that our attitude towards Falstaff is by no means the same as it was when we were first making his acquaintance: we have learned to love the old rascal, though we still recognize the fact that he is an old rascal.

This humour of character, reaching its greatest height in such figures as Falstaff, is itself the richest and wisest kind of humour, sweetening and mellowing life for us. In England it ripens like the apple.

That is one way of linking humour and the English character. Here is another. Humour has been well defined as "thinking in fun while feeling in earnest." The English do not approach life intellectually; they do not demand that it shall conform to some rigid mental plan; they are not convinced that the universe can be penetrated by thought; they look askance at those grand first principles that seem to some alien peoples the very foundations of the world; they are willing to go to work, either in politics or art, without a theory to sustain them; and when they are more practical than other races, it is not—as those races frequently conclude—because they are coldly clear-sighted and unimaginative, but because they do not busy themselves asking reason to find a key when instinct has already shown them that the door is wide open. Thus, if they should think at all, they are quite likely to do a great deal of "thinking in fun." On the other hand, the English float through life on a deep if narrow stream of feeling; they commonly live in a matriarchy of the heart, unlike some other more effusive races, who flaunt the heart as if it were some new mistress and use the emotions to decorate some purely rational scheme of life; they live in such a deep intimacy with their feelings that they find it difficult and distasteful to reveal them; they have a horror of pretended feeling or easy emotion just because feeling to them is the key to the inner citadel, and to lose control of themselves is to reveal the last secret. Thus, when they are feeling at all, they are generally "feeling in earnest." And if humour is thinking in fun while feeling in earnest, there should be humour in England.

George Meredith used to ask: "Is it accepted of song?" He proposed song as a test. If your feelings survived the ordeal of sustaining a good sonnet, then they were worth having, were genuine and noble. This is only a companion test to that other which we have long imposed: is it accepted of humour? We ask that men and ideas and art shall survive the ordeal of laughter. That is why we in England have had so much burlesque and parody, neither of which has ever injured good work but has always been fatal to bad. In no other country will you hear so much talk about a sense of humour. "But has he a sense of humour?" we are always asking one another. It is a question that irritates some people, and we remember a very angry preface by one of the best of our younger poets, Mr. Robert Nichols, in which he calls a sense of humour a bogey. "Slay humour ere humour slays you," he cries to his degenerate grinning countrymen; and would seem to be trying to make them afraid of ever seeing a joke again. But being a good Englishman and a good artist, Mr. Nichols is no enemy to real humour, as he very quickly shows by talking very well about it in this same preface: he tells us that the function of humour is "to twitch the self-elected by the sleeve, shake its bells, hold up its mirror at an awkward angle, and ask his master how he likes his image"; and then later he declares that humour "is a tonic medicine, restoring clouded or overweening fancies to clarity." What he was really objecting to is the sniggering on unimaginative persons, and it is a pity he did not say so. But if Mr. Nichols or anyone else told us that we talk too much about humour, we ought to have our reply ready. "Learned men, brother Toby, don't write dialogues upon long noses for nothing!" Nor do we talk about a sense of humour for nothing. From what we have seen of the English character, we can easily imagine—even if we had not observed the fact—that the Englishman without humour is in a worse case than the solemn specimen of some other nationality. Governed, as he is, by that inner atmosphere, that weather in the soul; if there is no sense of humour to keep in check his egoism, his ponderous vanity, his intellectual wilfulness, then they will be left to run riot. Mr. Podsnap and Sir Willoughby Patterne are capital examples of the Englishman without humour; and no other race could have spawned these solemn monsters. We must remember Mr. Santayana's remark: "Nowhere do we come oftener upon those two social abortions, the affected and the disaffected." We all know them, and, as they usually travel a good deal, the observant foreigner knows them too, and imagines they are typical. What he does not know is that they are typical of England outside its state of grace, of the English mind unleavened by humour; and that he is really seeing *Hamlet* without the Prince, the butts without the host of marksmen. He forgets that if we have more unsmiling oddities than other nations, we have also more people fully capable of enjoying whatever plumed idiocies they may bring forth. You will find Justice Shallow and Cousin Silence prattling and numbling together somewhere in this island. But you will also find Jack Falstaff there too, laughing at them.

CHAPTER II

CLOWNS AND COMEDIANS

THE English people have always adored clowns and comedians. As soon as a stage was set up in this country, there was fooling. Even in our mediæval mysteries, humour is for ever breaking in. *The Deluge* turns Noah's wife into a shrew, who refuses to enter the Ark and belabours the patriarch. The *Wakefield Shepherds' Play* has some comic business concerned with sheep-stealing in it, and introduces two characters, Mak and his wife, who have nothing to do with any biblical narrative, but have a great deal to do with Yorkshire then and now. Herod himself becomes a comic character, a forefather of Ancient Pistol. Even the devils and demons are droll; the *Trial of Joseph and Mary* is full of low comedy; and *Doomsday* is turned into a roaring farce. These mysteries were for the most part performed by artisans on holiday, who did not scruple to take most of the mystery out of them and put in jokes and droll topical allusions and horseplay. They gave Bottom the Weaver his chance. Then came the moralities, the interludes, and the early crude plays, and drollery found its way into all of them, as we know from surviving examples of these various dramatic forms. Once the Elizabethan Theatre came into its existence, with professional players dependent on the support of the public, there was no suppressing the comedian. What the ordinary playgoers liked was a mixture of blood and thunder and clowning, and they were not to be baulked. All historians of Elizabethan drama have recognized this fact and have pointed out its significance. The professional playwright had to consider these tastes and therefore was compelled to work along certain lines. Solemn young men from the Universities, who were not really very different from our solemn young graduates except that they were called "wits" and not "highbrows," were anxious that the English drama should model itself upon Latin tragedy, but the public had other views and the professional dramatists were compelled to share them. To this simple fact we owe our possession of the colossal and enchanted world of Shakespeare.

Shakespeare grumbled, of course, like any dramatist who knows that he is at the mercy of his leading players. These were chiefly clowns and comedians, and they had a habit of "gagging." That is why Hamlet, transformed for the moment into an anxious dramatist, is made to say: "Let those that play your clowns speak no more than is set down for them," though the speech is really in character, for we may see in it the vain hope of the idealist. The attitude of the ordinary Elizabethan playgoer is exactly set forth in a speech by Simon the Tanner, Mayor of Queenborough, in Middleton's comedy of that name:

O, the clowns that I have seen in my time!
The very peeping out of one of them would have
made a young heir laugh, though his father lay

a-dying; a man undone in law the day before (the saddest case that can be) might for his twopence have burst himself with laughing, and ended all his miseries. Here was a merry world, my masters!

> Some talk of things of state, of puling stuff;
> There's nothing in a play to a clown, if he
> Have the grace to hit on't; that's the thing
> indeed:
> The king shows well, but he sets off the
> king. . . .

And here Simon speaks for all our countrymen who have crowded into pits and galleries these last few centuries. "O, the clowns that I have seen in my time!" How often have we heard that cry and warmed to it! It was the clowns and comedians (they were sometimes Court jesters too) who were first favourites of Elizabethan audiences: Will Summer, Richard Tarlton, Will Kemp were the best known of all. Men like Tarlton (whose *Jests* were published in 1611) and Kemp not only played parts, but gave what we should call "turns" in the intervals, when they sang and joked and danced. When Shakespeare first came to London, Raleigh tells us, "Tarlton's pipe and tabor, his monologues and impromptus and jigs, were the delight of the public. . . . One of these jigs, wherein each of the short verses was satirically directed at this or that member of the audience, has the refrain: "So pipeth the crow, Sitting upon a wall—Please one and please all." Peering through the mist of centuries, we can see him jigging away, a vague and antique figure of fun.

But if we want to discover him all alive and roaring, short verses, refrain, jokes and jigs, nothing wanting, we have only to walk into the nearest music hall.

This clown of Elizabethan drama who, like his modern successor, the comedian, frankly exploited a humorous personality, is a very English figure. Towards the end of the period, when genteel comedy made its appearance, he was driven out to make room for the comic actor, who merely played the part of the intriguing servant (a foreign type) and similar parts, such as we find in the comedies of Beaumont and Fletcher. The latter was congratulated on the superiority of his comedy:

Shakespeare to thee was dull, whose best wit lies
I' the ladies' questions and the ools' replies,
Old-fashioned wit, which walk'd from town to town
In trunk-hose, which our fathers call'd the clown.

This new style, which banished coarse humour to bring in dirty wit, pleased the upper classes, the gentry of the Court; but both new and old, wit and humour, displeased that powerful section of the public, chiefly belonging to the middle classes, known as the Puritans, who, once they were in power, kept the theatres closed. Meanwhile, the ordinary people, the English crowd, who were not Puritans, had not changed at all; they were the same people at heart who had laughed at Tarlton, and who were later to laugh at Munden and Dan Leno. And here we must stop to honour one, Robert Cox, for it was he who, during the period when the theatres were closed and all play-acting suppressed, organized bands of strolling players and devised certain entertainments that purported to be merely exhibitions of rope-dancing and the like but that actually included a great many famous comic scenes, and among them the Falstaff scenes. These were put together and, under the name of *Humours* and *Drolleries*, were afterwards published for the use of theatrical booths at fairs. Let us be grateful to Robert Cox, because he kept Falstaff and Hostess Quickly in the sack and sugar of public laughter and applause during a season of dearth. Even when the theatres were opened again, these *Humours* and *Drolleries* must have been seen for many a year at fairs or wherever the strolling troups appeared; and thus it is likely that for some time the English common people (who deserved it) had better fun at their command than the King and his Court. But at times, however, their tastes agreed. "The truth is," says Pepys, writing of Dryden's new play, "there is a comical part done by Nell, which is Florimell, that I never can hope ever to see the like done again by man—or woman. The King and the Duke were at the play. But so great performance of a comical part was never, I believe, in the world before as Nell do this. . . ." No king's mistress was ever such a favourite with the people of England as Nell Gwynne. But then she was one of themselves: she had humour.

The comic scenes in the Restoration Theatre must have been very dirty, for we know what Dryden and his fellows could do in the matter of text, and even then we must make further allowance for the players, who did not demand such situations and passages for nothing. The taste of the general public, as distinct from the rakes and women of the town, was not in favour of such extremes of licence. Early in Anne's reign, the censorship was in force, as the following proclamation, dated March 1704, clearly shows:

> Whereas great Complaints have been made to Her Majesty, of many indecent profane and immoral Expressions that are usually spoken by Players and Mountebanks contrary to Religion and Good Manners. And thereupon Her Majesty has lately given Order to *Charles Killigrew, Esqre.*; Her Majesty's Master of the Revels, to take especial care to correct all such Abuses. The said Master of the Revels does therefore hereby require all Stage Players, Mountebanks, and all other Persons, mounting Stages, or otherwise, to bring their Several Plays, Drolls, Farces, Interludes, Dialogues, Prologues, and other Entertainments, fairly written, to him at his Office in *Somerset House,* to be by him perused, corrected and allow'd under his hand, pursuant to Her Majesty's Command. . . .

There are, too, numerous complaints in the *Tatler* and *Spectator*, both against the players and the audiences. An advertisement of a benefit performance suggests a programme not unlike that of a modern music-hall:

> For the Benefit of Will. Bullock.
> At the Theatre Royal in Drury Lane, on Whitsun Monday, being the 5th of June, will be

reviv'd the Diverting Comedy call'd the Miser.
Written by the Author of the Squire of Alsatia;
the part of Timothy Sqeez the Scriveners foolish
Son to be acted by Will. Bullock. With Entertainments of Dancing by Monsieur du Ruell. And
Mr. Clinch of Barnet will perform these several
performances, first an Organ, with Three Voices,
then the Double Curtel, the Flute, the Bells, the
Huntsman, the Horn, and Pack of Dogs, all with
his mouth; and an old Woman of Fourscore
Years of Age nursing her Grand Child; all of
which he does open on the Stage. Next a Gentleman will perform several Mimick Entertainments
on the Ladder, first he stands on the top round
with a Bottle in one hand and a Glass in the other,
and drinks a Health; then plays several Tunes on
the Violin, with fifteen other surprising Performances which no man but himself can do. And
Will Pinkeman will dance the Miller's Dance and
speak a comical joking Epilogue on an Ass.
Beginning exactly at five a Clock by reason of the
length of the Entertainments. At Common
Prices.

Will Bullock and Will Pinkeman (Penkethman)
were two of the best low comedy actors of the time.
More important, of course, was the famous Colley
Cibber—"A Gentleman of his time who was Arriv'd to
an exceeding Perfection, in hitting justly the Humour
of a starcht Beau or Fop; as the *Lord Fopington*; *Sir
Fopling* and *Sir Courtly*." A still better comedian was
Doggett, whose Coat and Badge are still raced for by
the Thames watermen, and of whom it was said:

"On the Stage, he's very Aspectabund, wearing Farce in his face, his Thoughts deliberately framing his Utterance Congruous to his Looks; He is the only Comick Original now extant." Doggett, like Bullock and Pinkeman and many of the other comedians, ran a booth at Bartholomew Fair. And a word must be spared for John Rich, who was called "the father of English pantomime," for under the name of Lun he played Harlequin in an entertainment that developed into an annual pantomime. He excelled in the drollery of dumb show, as Garrick's tribute tells us:

When Lun appeared, with matchless art and whim,
He gave the power of speech to every limb:
Tho' masked and mute, conveyed his quick intent,
And told in frolic gesture what he meant.

The greatest comedian of the eighteenth century, however, was probably Samuel Foote, mimic, buffoon, wit, and comic dramatist, Even Dr. Johnson, who detested players and had threatened Foote with a thrashing if he should mimic him, admitted to a numerous company (among whom was Wilkes, another man that Johnson could not dislike because of his high spirits) that Foote was not to be resisted.

We have a hundred examples of his ready wit. When a well-known gambler had complained to him of being thrown out of a window at Bath, and had asked what he should do to repair his injured honour, Foote replied instantly: "Do? Why, 'tis a plain case, never play so high again as long as you live." A rich doctor, setting up his carriage, asked Foote's advice on the choice of a motto. "What is your crest?" said Foote. "Three mallards," replied the doctor. "Why, then," said Foote, "the motto I would recommend to you is *Quack, quack, quack*." He was once in company when the talk turned on the mutability of the world. "Can you account for this?" said a master builder who was sitting next to him. "Why, not very clearly," Foote answered, "except we could suppose the world was built by contract." He could never resist the temptation. When his friend, Sir Francis Blake Delavel, died, Foote was so overcome that he saw nobody for three days. On the fourth day, his treasurer called to see him on urgent business, and Foote, still tearful, inquired when Sir Francis was to be buried. "Not till the latter end of the next week, sir," the treasurer replied, "as I hear the surgeons intend first to dissect his head." "And what will they get there?" Foote cried, his face still wet with tears. "I'm sure I have known Frank these five and twenty years, and I never could find anything in it."

Foote, an Oxford man and not ill read, was originally intended for the Bar and spent some years in the Temple, during which period he contrived to go through more than one fortune. When he turned actor, he tried tragedy and then genteel comedy, but was not very successful, and so finally invented a new kind of entertainment that gave him an opportunity of displaying his powers as a mimic. Not only did he burlesque certain well-known characters of the town, but he also burlesqued a number of his fellow actors. The victims promptly took measures to have the entertainment suppressed, but Foote ingeniously countered by evading the licensing laws of the theatre. He immediately issued an invitation "to his friends and the public" to drink tea with him at the Haymarket Theatre the following morning at noon: "And 'tis hoped there will be a great deal of comedy and some joyous spirits; he will endeavour to make the morning as diverting as possible. N.B.—*Sir Dilbury Diddle will be there, and Lady Betty Frisk has absolutely promised.*" When the audience were assembled, Foote came forward and told them that he was training some young actors, and, while tea was being made, would proceed with his instructions to his pupils. The joke was so successful that he gave this and similar entertainments for many years. Everybody who has read Boswell will remember that Dr. Johnson was to have been one of the victims of Foote's satire and mimicry, and that Foote changed his mind when he heard that the stout doctor had bought an enormous oak cudgel and intended to plant himself in the front row on the first night. Curiously enough, the victim who was chosen to take Johnson's place in the farce (*The Orators*) was a pompous but otherwise inoffensive printer, who happened to have a wooden leg; and not long afterwards Foote himself, having been tricked into riding a dangerously spirited horse, fractured and finally lost one of his own legs. This misfortune, however, did not prevent him from acting, and he even contrived to turn it to good uses. He wrote a large number of farces for his own theatre, and though they were hastily written and badly constructed, they have some genuine comic scenes and some really ridiculous characters, most of which were played, of course, by Foote himself. Here is his Major Sturgeon of the Middlesex Militia, in *The Mayor of Garratt*. He is discovered talking of his military experiences to his friend, Sir Jacob Jollop:

Major S.—Oh, such marchings and counter-marchings, from Brentford to Ealing, from Ealing to Acton, from Acton to Uxbridge; the dust flying, sun scorching, men sweating! Why, there was our last expedition to Hounslow; that day's work carried off Major Molossas. Bunhill-fields never saw a braver commander! He was an irreparable loss to the Service.

Sir J.—How came that about?

Major S.—Why, it was partly the major's own fault; I advised him to pull off his spurs before he went into action; but he was resolute, and would not be ruled.

Sir J.—Spirit; zeal for the Service.

Major S.—Doubtless. But to proceed: in order to get our men in good spirits, we were quartered at Thistleworth, the evening before. At day-break, our regiment formed at Hounslow, town's-end, as it might be about here. The major made a fine disposition: on we marched, the men all in high spirits, to attack the gibbet where Gardel is hanging; but turning down a narrow lane to the left, as it might be about there, in order to possess a pig-sty, that we might take the gallows in flank, and, at all events, secure a retreat, who should come by but a drove of fat oxen from Smithfield. The drums beat in the front, the dogs barked in the rear, the oxen set up a gallop; on they came thundering upon us, broke through our ranks in an instant, and threw the whole corps in confusion.

Sir J.—Terrible!

Major S.—The major's horse took to his heels; away he scoured over the heath. The gallant commander stuck both spurs into his flank, and for some time, held by his mane, but in crossing a ditch, the horse threw up his head, gave the major a douse in the chaps, and plumped him into a gravel-pit, just by the powder-mills.

Sir J.—Dreadful!

Major S.—Why, as Captain Cucumber, Lieutenant Puttyman, Ensign Tripe, and myself, were returning to town in the Turnham-green stage, we were stopped near the Hammersmith turnpike, and robbed and stripped by a single footpad.

Sir J.—An unfortunate day, indeed.

Major S.—But, in some measure, to make me amends, I got the major's commission.

Sir J.—You did?

Major S.—O yes. I was the only one of the corps that could ride; otherwise we always succeeded of course; no jumping over heads, no underhand work among us; all men of honour; and I must do the regiment the justice to say, there never was a set of more amiable officers.

Sir J.—Quiet and peaceable.

Major S.—As lambs, Sir Jacob. Excepting one

c

boxing-bout at the Three Compasses, in Acton, between Captain Sheers and the colonel, concerning a game at all-fours, I don't remember a single dispute.

Sir J.—Why, that was mere mutiny; the captain ought to have been broke.

Major S.—He was; for the colonel not only took away his cockade, but his custom; and I don't think poor Captain Sheers has done a stitch for him since.

Such a part as this, played by a comedian of genius, must have been irresistible. "Sir, he does not make fools of his company," said Dr. Johnson, talking of Foote; "they whom he exposes are fools already: he only brings them into action." Mimic and buffoon though he was, Samuel Foote cannot be denied his little place among the English humorists.

Another step—though without taking leave of Major Sturgeon—and we are in the next age, with Hazlitt. We can catch him praising this very play, the *Mayor of Garratt*, which he calls Foote's *magnum opus* and "one of the best acted farces that we have." At last the comic stage has its critical and eloquent admirers. If literary tributes are any criterion, then the theatre of the Regency excels in drollery. It was probably no better or worse than any other, but it was fortunate in having that blest pair of sirens, Lamb and Hazlitt, in constant attendance and only too eager to praise. The old actors wander through their essays; Jack Bannister and Dodd and Dicky Suett haunt them as the sounding cataract haunted

their friend Wordsworth. Liston was Hazlitt's
favourite comic actor:

> Mr. Liston has more comic humour, more
> power of face, and a more genial and happy vein
> of folly, than any other actor we remember. His
> farce is not caricature; his drollery oozes out of
> his features, and trickles down his face: his voice
> is a pitch-pine for laughter. He does some
> characters but indifferently, others respectably;
> but when he *puts himself whole* into a jest, it is un-
> rivalled. Munden with all his merit, his whim,
> his imagination, and with his broad effects, is a
> caricaturist in the comparison. . . .

Munden, with his whim and his imagination, was,
of course, Lamb's man, though Lamb was ready to
praise all the comedians of any merit he had ever
set eyes on. There must have been a grotesquerie of
humour in Munden that captured Lamb's imagination, and that imagination has conferred immortality
upon the comedian. Having Lamb's essay on the
acting of Munden, we need not regret never having
seen the man himself, for here is his apotheosis, all
the humour of him caught and then enriched by
being passed through that delicate wild imagination.

> Can any man *wonder*, like him? Can any man
> *see ghosts*, like him? or fight with *his own shadow*—
> "Sessa"—as he does in that strangely-neglected
> thing, the *Cobbler of Preston*—where his alterations
> from the Cobbler to the Magnifico, and from the
> Magnifico to the Cobbler, keep the brain of the

spectator in as wild a ferment, as if some Arabian Night were being acted before him. Who like him can throw, or ever attempted to throw, a preternatural interest over the commonest daily-life objects. A table, or a joint stool, in his conception, rises into a dignity equivalent to Cassiopeia's Chair. It is invested with constellatory importance. You could not speak of it with more deference, if it were mounted into the firmament. A beggar in the hands of Michael Angelo, says Fuseli, rose the Patriarch of Poverty. So the gusto of Munden antiquates and ennobles what it touches. His pots and his ladles are as grand and primal as the seething-pots and hooks seen in old prophetic vision. A tub of butter, contemplated by him, amounts to a Platonic idea. He understands a leg of mutton in its quiddity. He stands wondering, amid the commonplace materials of life, like primeval man with the sun and stars about him.

And why should not Talfourd's story of Lamb at Munden's last performance have a place here? Is it not full of the thing these chapters are trying to describe?

On the last night of his (Munden's) appearance, Lamb was very desirous to attend, but every place in the boxes had long been secured; and Lamb was not strong enough to stand the tremendous rush, by enduring which, alone, he could hope to obtain a place in the pit; when Munden's gratitude for his exquisite praise anticipated his wish, by providing for him and Miss Lamb places in a corner of the orchestra, close to the stage. The play of the *Poor Gentleman* in which Munden played "Sir Robert Bramble," had concluded, and the audience were impatiently waiting for the farce, in which the great comedian was to delight them for the last time, when my attention was suddenly called to Lamb by Miss Kelly, who sat with party far withdrawn into the obscurity of one of the upper boxes, but overlooking the radiant hollow which waved below us, to our friend. In his hand, directly beneath the line of stagelights, glistened a huge porter-pot, which he was draining; while the broad face of old Munden was seen thrust out from the door by which the musicians enter, watching the close of the draught, when he might receive and hide the portentous beaker from the gaze of the admiring neighbours. Some unknown benefactor had sent four pots of stout to keep up the veteran's heart during his last trial; and, not being able to drink them all, he bethought him of Lamb, and without considering the wonder which would be excited in the brilliant crowd who surrounded him, conveyed himself the cordial chalice to Lamb's parched lips.

This is the moment to take leave of them both, the greatest droll and the greatest humorist of their age, while they are still down there in the orchestra, undisturbed by the winks and nudges of the fashionable crowd, smiling at one another over a gargantuan pot of porter.

We will recall Munden, however, just to tell him that if he had flourished at the end instead of at the beginning of the last century, he would probably have been one of the great drolls of the "Halls." He was obviously not so much a comic actor, conscientiously presenting an amusing part, but a real comedian, exploiting his own rich personality, to whom a part was a mere excuse for appearing on the stage. Comedians of this kind—true descendants of Elizabethan Tarlton and Kemp—have always been the idols of the English people, who prefer a droll chunk of personality to comic acting. They do not like a comedian to be always different, but to be for ever himself, or, if you will, to be more himself each time they see him. It was some time before the music-hall proper developed out of those tavern sing-songs, the Cave of Harmony that Colonel Newcombe visited, the Harmonic Meeting at the Sol's Arms described in *Bleak House*. There the fun was provided by a Little Swills:

The landlord of the Sol's Arms, finding Little Swills so popular, commends him highly to the Juryman and public; observing that, for a song in character, he don't know his equal, and that that man's character-wardrobe would fill a cart.

Thus gradually the Sol's Arms melts into the shadowy night, and then flares out of it strong in gas. The Harmonic Meeting hour arriving, the gentleman of professional celebrity takes the chair; is faced (red-faced) by Little Swills; their friends rally round them, and support first-rate talent. In the zenith of the evening, Little Swills

says, Gentlemen, if you'll permit me, I'll attempt
a short description of a scene of real life that came
off here to-day. Is much applauded and en-
couraged; goes out of the room as Swills; comes
in as the Coroner (not in the least in the world
like him); describes the Inquest, with recreative
intervals of pianoforte accompaniment to the
refrain—With his (the Coroner's) tippy tol li
doll, tippy tol lo doll, tippy tol li doll, Dee!

Then came the era of the Lion Comique, the be-
whiskered masher, George Leybourne and his
Champagne Charlie, the "Great Vance" with his:

> For they always go a-rolling home,
> They always go a-rolling home,
>   A jolly lot are they!
>   Tra la la, Tra la la.
> Slap bang, here we are again!
> Slap bang, here we are again!
> A jolly lot are we!

These are the sprees of yesteryear. If there was
humour in these things, it was no longer-lived than
the bubbles in the champagne that George Leybourne
sometimes gave his audiences: nothing now seems
so dreary as this determined jollity. The vulgarity
of this stuff, with its talk of "swells" and "British
gentlemen" (meaning, in truth, racing touts and
dashing bagmen), is very different from the so-called
vulgarity of the later "Halls," the real variety show
as distinct from the singing-room. The time came
when, we imagine, a Lamb would have preferred
the music-hall to the theatre. It achieved a humour

not so very different, at its best, from that of
Shakespeare's clowns. Out of the strong came forth
sweetness. Red noses, battered hats, a blaring
orchestra, and jokes about mother-in-law, the lodger,
kippers, beer, and cheese—the soil was coarse and
rank enough, but here and there it flowered into
something that Lamb would have clapped his hands
at, the humour of character. Touchstone and Sir
Toby Belch and Andrew Aguecheek and Ancient
Pistol popped up again, came from London side-
streets, put on big boots and concertina check
trousers, red wigs and redder noses, sang inane
choruses in hoarse Cockney voices and, as they
banged the stage with the ruin of an umbrella, took
delighted thousands into their confidence, opened
wide once more the doors of that Eastcheap tavern
and unknowingly conducted pilgrimages to Arden
and Illyria.

Thus, it became possible yet again for an essayist
to pay his tribute to a stage droll, as Mr. E. V.
Lucas did so generously and wisely to Dan Leno:

That was, perhaps, Dan Leno's greatest
triumph, that the grimy sordid material of the
music-hall low comedian, which, with so many
singers, remains grimy and sordid, and perhaps
even becomes more grimy and sordid, in his
refining hands became radiant, joyous, a legiti-
mate source of mirth. In its nakedness it was still
drunkenness, quarrelsomeness, petty poverty;
still hunger, even crime; but such was the native
cleanness of this little, eager, sympathetic observer and reader of life, such was his gift of

showing the comic, the unexpected, side, that it emerged the most suitable, the gayest joke. He might be said to have been a crucible that transmuted mud to gold.

That was Dan Leno. And there were others: Chevalier and Gus Elen and Marie Lloyd, who represented the sardonic wit and gusty laughter and all the rich vitality of the London streets. We still have our drolls, though the golden age of the "Halls" has already receded and the modern comedian is more likely to be found in the bright wilderness of revue and musical comedy. We make no apology for mentioning these contemporaries here, even though there is so much to be said, so many greater names to be brought in, even though opinions may differ as to their merit as drolls. This kind of humour can only be caught on the wing; it is the laughter that was ringing last night that tells us where the English are actually finding their fun; and the least of these must mean more to us than Johnson's Foote or Lamb's Munden.

There is George Robey, with his gestures and grimaces that hint at unutterable things, his air of outraged dignity when he hears the shout of laughter; he always presents the same character, a Trinculo with a dash of Brother Stiggins, a Silenus from some dingy suburb. There is W. H. Berry, who transforms the vague characters of musical comedy into great creatures out of Illyria, at once impudent and timid, keeping one eye on the cakes and ale and the other on some virago of a wife. There is A. W. Baskcomb, once the most melancholy

of the pirates in *Peter Pan*, who now takes his disillusion, a voice like the very croak of despair, a
figure bent with resignation, into the brittle gaieties
of revue and musical comedy, and these gaieties,
this unreal brightness, collapse at his approach but
are then instantly transmuted into genuine humour.
There is Leslie Henson, who is a dynamo of the
ridiculous and contrives to look like all the silly
people we have ever met and then soars into the blue
of absurd caricature, so that we are reminded of
nothing less than the Fish footman and the Frog
footman in *Alice in Wonderland*. There is Miss Maisie
Gay, who, with the most devastating burlesque, will
give you any and every kind of middle-aged woman,
from the fatuous ballad-singer, alternately glaring
at the accompanist and smiling at the audience, to
the shabby-genteel drab with a sniff and a watery eye,
and who is able, when she thinks fit, to add to her
humour a fleeting sense of pathos. Here, then, are
some of our own drolls, and the reader who does not
find these to his taste may substitute his own
favourites: it is enough that we, too, can say with
the Mayor of Queenborough: "O, the clowns that
I have seen in my time."

There is still left us the greatest clown in the
world, the little man whose face and figure and
characteristic gestures and grimaces would be
instantly recognized anywhere in Europe and
America, and in a good slice of Asia, wherever, in
fact, the moving pictures have gone. Room must
be found here for Charles Chaplin, emperor of the
comic shadows. In him we have a Cockney droll
who has conquered the world. He spent his boy-

hood in the London streets, those crowded East End streets that are as full of tragi-comedy, of rapid alternations of disaster and buffoonery, as an Elizabethan play. He graduated as a mime in the English music-halls. When he became a film actor he was for some time nothing but a minor buffoon, compelled to indulge in the conventional absurdities, but it was not long before he stood apart from the other film comedians because he created an amusing and original figure, the little man with the mop of curly hair and tiny moustache, the bowler and walking-stick, the short coat, baggy trousers and big boots, the "Charlie" known all over the world. At first the adventures of this figure—representing at that time a penniless but ingenious adventurer—were not very different from those of other film buffoons, though it was very soon obvious that Chaplin's art was more highly finished than that of his fellow comedians, better adapted to the peculiar conditions of film work, which demands that everything should be conveyed through the eye, that a lifted eyebrow, a turn of the head, or a mere shrugging, should mean as much as two or three speeches on the stage. But when the comedian himself, instead of simply playing his own part, began to devise the whole entertainment, buffoonery was transmuted into humour, and the Chaplin films, with their richness and subtlety, were raised above all other comic films. There was more laughter than before, but now it was something more than derisive yelling and idle guffawing: sometimes, indeed, as you watched the grotesque little figure go shambling and capering on its way, vainly trying to dodge the thwacks of circumstance, you felt an affectionate concern and your laughter, when it came, was half a relief from tears. Affection and a touch of pathos transformed the clowning into humour. And now, "Charlie" was no longer the penniless adventurer, the traditional "broken-down swell" of music-hall sketches, but rather the quaint representative of those millions of the poor who may be found in all our great cities and who seem to be for ever fighting hopefully a losing battle with Fate; not the grim proletariat of the communist tracts nor yet the apathetic herd seen by the sociologist, but the living people, quick to laughter and tears, who are nourished by odd dreams as they contrive to exist so long and hopefully on the very edge of disaster. These are the people that Dickens saw, the little clerks and shopkeepers, and the "Charlie" of the pictures is not unlike a Dickens character, a Dick Swiveller or a Mr. Wilfer. And just as there is in Dickens an implied or unconscious pathos that is much better than his deliberate pathos, so, too, in some recent Chaplin films, which have not been improved by the insertion of definitely pathetic incidents, there has been a fine indirect pathos, the dumb pathos of the crowd. There is no art more cosmopolitan than this of the films. Where Charles Chaplin lives and works, the nations gather to make their shadow shows. But we cannot help thinking that it was not for nothing that he once played and dreamed in the London streets, that there is something significant in this suggestion of the Dickens spirit in his drollery. There is humour here and the best of it is of a kind we knew of old, however new the art that presents it may be. The world's great clown is an English humorist.

We have said more about the actors than the audience, but the quality of one tells us of the quality of the other. That Mayor of Queenborough in the play speaks for all of us; we have long loved laughter in the theatre, and especially the laughter that is tempered and mellowed by affection and a hint of tears; we may not bring the sharpest of wits to the comedian who is the satirist and critic, but we can dote on him who goes a step further and shows us Brother Fool. When Christopher Sly, a typical Englishman, wakes up to find a wife at his elbow and a play about to begin, he makes no more ado but says:

> Well, we'll see't.
> Come, madam wife, sit by my side,
> And let the world slip: we shall ne'er be younger.

And so speaks for all of us. He does not know exactly who he is or where he is, like most of us, but some things he knows, and there is in his little speech both good philosophy and good humour. He well deserved the play they gave him, just as the English people, themselves so often full of good philosophy and good humour, have well deserved both the play and Christopher Sly.

CHAPTER III

COMIC ART

HAZLITT put Hogarth among his *English Comic Writers*. Thackeray treats him as one of the English humorists of the eighteenth century and gives him a place alongside Smollett and Fielding. Lamb said that Hogarth's prints "are analogous to the best novels of Smollett and Fielding." Hazlitt went further, so far, indeed, that it is not easy to follow him. He is comparing Hogarth with Wilkie:

There is not a single picture of his (Hogarth's) containing a representation of merely natural or domestic scenery. He is carried away by a passion for the *ridiculous*. His object is not so much "to hold the mirror up to nature" as "to show vice her own feature, scorn her own image." He is so far contenting himself with still-life that he is always on the verge of caricature, though without ever falling into it. He does not represent folly or vice in its incipient, or dormant, or *grub* state; but full-grown, with wings, pampered into all sorts of affectation, airy, ostentatious, and extravagant. Folly is there seen at the height—the moon is at the full; it is "the very error of the time." There is a perpetual collision of eccentricities—a tilt and tournament of absurdities; the prejudices and caprices of mankind are let loose, and set together by the ears, as in a bear-garden. Hogarth paints

nothing but comedy or tragi-comedy. Wilkie
paints neither one nor the other. Hogarth never
looks at any object but to find out a moral or a
ludicrous effect. Wilkie never looks at any object
but to see that it is there. Hogarth's pictures are
a perfect jest-book from one end to the other. . . .
In looking at Hogarth, you are ready to burst your
sides with laughing at the unaccountable jumble
of odd things which are brought together. . . .

It is hard to resist such enthusiastic advocacy, but
truth compels us to ask ourselves whether we are
in practice ready to burst our sides with laughing at
these pictures and prints. Are they really so irresistible as Hazlitt would appear to think they are? We
do not, of course, refer to such grim moralities as
The Idle and the Industrious Apprentices, *The Harlot's
Progress*, and *The Rake's Progress*, nor even to the
elaborate satires of *Marriage à la Mode*, but to such
plates as *The Cockpit*, *The Sleeping Congregation*, the
Election and *Time of Day*, none of which make any
pretence of being pictorial sermons. Do we find in
these things "the keenest and happiest humour"?
It is true they have a magnificent exuberance; they
show us life charged to the full with animal vitality
and so perhaps become comic; and we are compelled
to admit their realism, strong and rank and earthy.
But at this remove, we find in these prints a great
deal of the grotesque and very little of the purely
humorous. He has been compared with Fielding and
Smollett. But now we do not put these two novelists
on the same level: we recognize that Fielding was
unquestionably the superior, a genuine humorist and

a creator of character. Smollett worked on the surface of life, finding his fun in grotesque appearances and horseplay: he made the world grin through a horse collar. And he did clumsily in words what Hogarth, with a better medium, did perfectly in lines and dots. But Hogarth cannot reach the inward humour, depending on ideas, showing the radical inconsistencies of this life, that we may find in Fielding. As humorists there can be no comparison between the two men.

An artist can achieve humour by a native drollery of vision, by holding up to the face of nature a curiously distorted mirror of his own. Some artists can make every line they draw resemble an absurd remark. But Hogarth is a perfectly serious artist; his pencil, so to speak, never moves drolly over the paper; and his is not so much comic art as pictorial satire. What he does is to illustrate a literary satire or moral tale that is not there and does not need to exist because the illustrator has contrived—and it is in the range, the ingenuity, the force of his contrivance that Hogarth is matchless—to say everything himself. He makes his point over and over again, and at the same time gives you the whole bustling scene, a complete picture of the age. His contemporaries were compelled to admit the force of his satire and the variety and truth of his representation. Posterity could admire all this and had the additional pleasure of capturing, through his works, a former age. Lamb and Hazlitt found in them a colossal eighteenth-century comedy for the eye, and praised so heartily (and, on the whole, justly) what had given them so many subjects for meditation or pleasant musing. No other English artist has given us such a complete world.

The comic art of the latter half of the eighteenth century is largely that of caricature. Gillray is first, Rowlandson second, and Sandby, Collet, Sayer, Bunbury, and Woodward may be all mentioned as being in the race. This was the era of John Bull, whose broad fist we seem to see in all the drawings of the period. The English do not appear to have had any nerves but only immense appetites and corresponding immensities of vitality and strength; a caricature has not a point but a felling blow from a cudgel; all foreigners are depicted as if they were apes; the humour is like the charge of a bull. But Gillray must be set apart from the other comic draughtsmen of his time. His genius rises far above a mere coarse strength and gusto. He has a grim humour of his own, but what distinguishes him, apart from his magnificent technique, is a malice at once so shrewd and passionate that it has a touch of sublimity about it. It was a bad day's work for George III when he made a lasting enemy of Gillray, as we are told he did when he refused to look at the sketches Gillray had made for Loutherbourg's picture of the Siege of Valenciennes. Never was any man, king or commoner, handled with more devastating malice. Gillray turns his Farmer George into a figure of farce. In the print, *Royal Affability*, we see the king, stupid and complacent, with a little tubby wife hanging on his arm, addressing a startled peasant who has just come from the pigs: "Well, friend, where a' you going, hay? What's your name, hay? Where do you live, hay? hay?" In another the

D

famous apple dumplings are introduced. We see a grinning old woman busy with her dumplings while the king, a glass to his eye, peers through the window and cries in astonishment: "Hay, hay? Apple dumplings? how get the apples in—how? Are they made without seams?" Equally bitter, of course, though not so successful, are Gillray's French Revolution and Napoleonic caricatures. One of the best of these is a droll little sketch of "Talleyrand, King-at-arms, bearing his master's genealogical tree, springing from Buone, Butcher," in which Talleyrand looks the old showman to the life. Gillray's greatest cartoons are not within our present range, and in purely social satire he was inferior to some of his contemporaries, notably Rowlandson. There is something peculiarly John Bullish about Rowlandson, and his work suggests better than any other the spirit of his age. It is as close to the earth as a farm-yard; his men are broad and beefy, and his women are all curves; the most delicate beauty in his illustrations would turn the scale at thirteen stone and be capable of eating a shoulder of mutton at one meal; and he turns all the characters in the novels he illustrated (including those of Sterne, Goldsmith, and Smollett) into huge farmers and overblown Covent Garden hussies. But there is about him a huge good-nature and rude health that does suggest the England he knew. He had its own boisterous humour. And there blows through all his work a fresh wind. He is obviously not the best artist to illustrate such a gentle little masterpiece as *The Vicar of Wakefield*, yet his drawings to that work, for all their faults, have some special virtues of their own, for they do at least take us out into the open air. We may be among drunken oafs and fat hussies, but nevertheless the sky is above our heads and there is grass beneath our feet.

This can hardly be said of the generation of comic artists that followed, men whose work is so familiar to us because we have seen so many of their illustrations to the novels of the period. These artists, George Cruikshank, Robert Seymour (for whose sake *Pickwick* was commissioned), "Phiz" (Hablot Knight Browne), and one or two others, were really widely different one from another in temperament and technique, as we soon discover if we examine their work properly; nevertheless when we compare their work as a whole with that which was done before or after their time, such differences are lost in a common likeness. All these illustrators seem to look at the same world. It is a world we have never seen ourselves, but, so strong is the influence of these artists (whose acquaintance we made when we first read Dickens), we cannot rid ourselves of the notion that this strange world does really represent the England of the period roughly between 1825 and 1845. The novels they illustrated have necessarily become part of this same world, a fact of considerable importance and one that literary criticism seems to have overlooked. Thus, most of us read Dickens first when we were children, at an age perhaps when a drawing tells us more than a page or two of print, and we saw his principal scenes and characters through the eyes of "Phiz" and Cruikshank; and no matter how many times we may have re-read him—perhaps deliberately avoiding the illustrations— it is doubtful if we have been able to rid ourselves of those first impressions. And certainly the whole atmosphere in which the lesser novelists of the time, such men as Lever and Harrison Ainsworth, now have their being for us would seem to have been created by their illustrators. Lever himself complained of being misrepresented: "Browne's sketches are as usual *caricatures*; they make my scenes too riotous and disorderly. The character of my books for uproarious people and incident I owe mainly to Master Phiz." On the other hand, it is necessary to point out that Dickens was more than satisfied with "Phiz," who was his friend and constant companion and was content to work under his author's direction in a way that more creative and forceful personalities, such as Cruikshank and Leech, would have found (and did find) too irksome. Moreover, the drawings came out of the age just as the novels did, and no doubt captured its spirit.

The world of these comic illustrators is quite different from that of Rowlandson, with its beefy men and blowsy women, open air and coarse earthiness. It is, to begin with, curiously indoor. Outdoor scenes there are in plenty, but somehow they do not look genuine; we feel we are looking at a stage scene, that the fields and the trees are daubed on a back-cloth. There is something dark and cramped about it. None of the people seem to be ordinary human beings, even grotesque human beings: they are all elfish. The streets are more crowded and uproarious than any streets we have ever seen in this world, crammed with the most fantastic out-at-elbows personages, like troupes of gnomes. There are no pretty, healthy women or robust and open-faced men. The women are either mere wisps or vast bundles of clothing; the men are either like tubs of butter or like be-whiskered and tightly clothed skeletons. It is a world of grotesques, illuminated not by the sun and moon but by the startling lights of the theatre, and for ever stirred by an elfish energy. It is significant that Cruikshank did his best work when he took leave of the real world altogether and turned to German fairy tales, which gave him the opportunity to run riot among giants and elves and devils. But he was always at his best when he was dealing with the frankly horrible—he was very much at home with *Oliver Twist*—or with that species of the comic grotesque that has horror only just round the corner. He had a magnificent sense of what we might call the Quaint; and even his very limitations as a draughtsman (he could never draw a horse, for example, and we see the same astonishing animal tumbling crazily through scores of his drawings) only seemed to establish him more firmly in his own special world. "Phiz" had many more limitations as a draughtsman and had far less original genius. None of his people seem to be made of bone and solid flesh; they look like marionettes, and usually like very fragile marionettes. Moreover, he was in the habit of repeating himself times without number. His docility, however, enabled him to work with the masterful Dickens, whose own ideas he contrived to represent with considerable success; and though there is little real humour in him, he might be called a master of comic atmosphere, who gives us strange glimpses of a region that is somewhere between England and Elfland.

John Leech takes us into England itself, though not without giving us many an elfish reminiscence. He forms a link between two schools of comic artists, for he was both the last of the illustrators and the first of the great *Punch* artists. He illustrated Dickens' *Christmas Carol* and *Battle of Life*, the *Handley Cross* novels, and a great many minor things, including the *Comic History of England* and the *Comic History of Rome*; and for over twenty years he worked hard for *Punch*. "There is no blinking the fact," wrote Thackeray, "that in Mr. Punch's cabinet John Leech is the right-hand man." There is no need to quote the praises of Thackeray and Dickens, both his friends, but it is worth remembering that Ruskin saw in Leech's sketches "the finest definition and natural history of the classes of our society, the kindest and subtlest analysis of its foibles, the tenderest flattery of its pretty and well-bred ways," that any artist had given us. Leech took comic art out of that region of the grotesque in which it had for so long existed, gave it gentleness and grace and good humour. His women and children are not divested of all prettiness in order that they may be funny. Indeed, his humour makes use of this very prettiness. The best of his work may be found in the innumerable tiny drawings, mere thumbnail sketches some of them, that he did for *Punch*, which can touch off with admirable humour—sometimes only with a few felicitous strokes—swells and footmen and loafers and sportsmen and stout shopkeepers and pretty girls and their patronizing young brothers. Perhaps he excelled in giving us the humours of family life in the middle classes. There is a characteristic little sketch of his, showing us a typical family on horseback with a grinning groom in attendance, called *A Freshener on the Downs*. Leech himself, however narrow his range might be or whatever his faults of draughtsmanship were, was a Freshener.

Now that we have arrived at *Punch*, whose generous volumes are easily our best storehouse of graphic humour, we had better call a halt in order to say something about the art itself. A great many of the artists who have appeared regularly in *Punch* are not comic artists at all, and only a very few have any claim to be considered humorists. Opening a volume of *Punch* drawings and jokes, we find these two specimens. On the left-hand page is a drawing of two ladies sitting in a drawing-room and looking at a pug, and below we read:

Lady Visitor—I see you still have poor old Bingo.
Fair Widow—Yes, I never look at him without thinking of poor dear Marmaduke!

The right-hand page shows us a sketch of a featureless young man being entertained at the tea-table by an equally featureless young woman. There is a dog in this drawing too, very prominent in the foreground, though it has nothing to do with the joke, which runs as follows:

He—And so, as I didn't know what the leopard would be up to next, I shot him on the spot.
She—How very exciting! And which spot did you shoot him on?

Now neither of these drawings gives the slightest assistance to the quip it illustrates; there is no fun in

them; they are perfectly serious pieces of illustration.
The only possible reason for their existence is that
they catch the eye and direct it to the jokes below;
though it seems incredible that an editor can have
wanted to call attention to the jests we have quoted.
The real comic artist, however, gives us a funny
drawing, immensely enlarging the joke he has
selected; and the more of a humorist he is, the less he
depends upon letterpress. Such artists may possibly
be inferior to their colleagues as draughtsmen, but,
nevertheless, they alone are important here. After
Leech, who was certainly a humorist, Keene holds
the field. Keene had not the humour of Leech, but
he had a finer technique and a magnificent sense of
comic character. His Scots and waiters and be-
whiskered volunteers and roistering "gents" and
cynical cabbies are presented with an astonishing
fidelity and force. For years, he and Du Maurier
(who was, as he himself said, the romantic tenor in
Punch's company, while Keene sang the comic songs
in his highly-trained basso) divided English social
life between them. Keene tended to specialize in the
middle and lower classes, while Du Maurier confined
himself to Society, satirizing the snobs and the
æsthetes. The latter had nothing like the vigour and
range of his colleague, who was undoubtedly the
greater artist; but it is far easier to forget the existence of Keene than it is to forget that of Du Maurier,
whose elongated aristocratic personages and favourite satirical characters, such as Sir Gorgius Midas
and Mrs. Ponsonby de Tomkyns, remain for us
types of the Society of the 'seventies and 'eighties.

This pictorial humour has its limitations. It

reproduces the weaknesses of its age. Alice Meynell, in her essay on *Victorian Caricature*, denounces it out of her outraged fastidiousness. A great deal of Victorian humour, she declares, had for its aim the vulgarizing of the married woman.

But if we examine the graphic humour of the period and also go through later collections of *Punch* drawings, we shall not imagine that Mrs. Meynell has laid a finger on the chief weakness. Our first thought will not be that Mr. Punch has been vulgar and coarsely unchivalrous. He has been that, at times, but always less so than current opinion in the street. The greatest weakness of his humour has always been its lack of ideas and what we must call for want of a better word—its snobbery. Here again, of course, Mr. Punch has never been more lacking in ideas and more snobbish than the vast majority of his readers; but we may justly argue that in these matters he ought to be ahead of them rather than abreast of them. He has made hundreds of jokes about hunting, for example, but these jokes nearly always turn on the mistakes of some ignorant beginner in the field, and not one of them ever penetrates the crust of ready-made opinion and shows us hunting as something absurd in itself. It is funny, no doubt, that a Frenchman should suggest shooting the fox, but it is even funnier that a number of our fellow countrymen should feel that their deepest feelings have been outraged by the suggestion. It is amusing when some ignorant new arrival, still unused to the social code of his hosts and fellow guests, should make an ass of himself in a drawing-room; but in the light of the truest humour, the whole assembly, rigid in their etiquette, could be seen as something absurd. The best humour goes to work by taking nothing for granted, by showing us ourselves, our habits, our antics, against the background of the night sky and the stars. Except on rare occasions, Mr. Punch has always taken most things—our etiquette, our social and moral code, our class distinctions, and the rest—for granted, and has been content to find his fun in the more superficial of our pretensions and embarrassments and failings. The other weakness, his occasional snobbery, is connected with this. In order to appreciate not a few of his jokes, you have to assume that servants, for example, exist in an entirely different world and are not made of the common human stuff, that there is something absurd in the fact that one of them should have received an offer of marriage or be interested in the fashions or exhibit the very same prejudices that are treated so tenderly in their masters. We do not find this weakness in a Dickens, whatever else he may have had in common with the comic artists who were his friends.

When we have taken leave of Du Maurier, through whose spectacles we still look at the Society of the 'seventies and 'eighties, we arrive at the 'nineties. There are many things that seem to us, at this remove, to be typical of the 'nineties, and among them are the drawings of Phil May. His work seems as characteristic of his decade (he was only in his middle twenties when it began and only outlived it by three years) as that of Beardsley. Although he was actually a Yorkshireman, we think of him as being in the van of the Cockney humorists—W. W.

Jacobs and Pett Ridge in the magazines, Albert
Chevalier and Marie Lloyd on the "halls"—who
suddenly marched into the limelight in the early
'nineties. This is not the place in which to discuss
his technique, famous for its fine economy of line,
but what it revealed is very much to our purpose,
for it was a vein of genuine humour. There was in
Phil May a very real sympathy with the people he
drew, the guttersnipes and costers and charwomen
and flower girls and seedy actors and be-feathered
"donahs," and there is his own enjoyment of their
gaiety and irony and humours in every line of his
best work. Thus he depended less than any of his
fellow artists on jokes and quips: there is fun enough
in his drawings, which frequently make the joke
themselves and always amplify it. A typical sketch
of his shows us a coster, brave in his "pearlies,"
with one hand to his mouth and with the other,
thumb out, pointing to his companion, a coster girl
dressed in her best. Beneath we read:

An Informal Introduction—'Arry (*shouting across
the street to his "Pal"*): "Hi! Bill! This is 'er!"

The drawing, sparkling with a kindly humour,
translates the two lines of letterpress into vivid life.
In the hands of another man it would be nothing.
But in 'Arry's face, in the very turn of his thumb, we
can see a droll mingling of the lover's pride with the
native irony of the East End male; and the face and
figure of the girl suggest a mixture of hauteur and
sheepishness. Another drawing shows us a coster
couple, gorgeous in their best, the girl with her
panoply of feathers and her frizzled hair, the man

with a loud check cap at the back of his head and a grin on his droll face, looking at themselves in a concave mirror: "I say, 'Arry, don't we look frights!" the girl is saying, her face wrinkling with laughter. There is real humour, not satire on the one hand nor buffoonery on the other, in every line of the drawing. As you laugh at 'Arry and his girl, you laugh at yourself, easily and without bitterness. Phil May died young but not before he had captured, once and for all in the annals of graphic humour, our little kingdom of Cockaigne.

We are now in our own age, and can do no more than hastily select a few names out of many and suggest a few qualities. There was good fun in Mr. E. T. Reed's "Prehistoric Peeps," and there was even better fun in the inimitable sketches of birds and animals by Mr. J. A. Shepherd, who could walk with his sketch-book through the Zoo and somehow contrive to satirize the whole human race without ever drawing one of its members. Mr. Heath Robinson discovered a vein of pure nonsense by sketching for us a world of his own, filled with learned-looking old gentlemen who are for ever engaged in performing simple operations in a very roundabout fashion by the use of fantastic machinery. Then there are the gloriously quiet absurdities of Mr. George Morrow, whose every line is somehow droll and whose little scenes from some odd history of his own are among the best things of our time. Nor must we forget the caricatures and cartoons of Mr. Max Beerbohm, who contrives to be a wit with the pencil as well as with the pen, though the chief excellence of his drawings, especially the superb series dealing with Rossetti and his circle, lies in their critical ideas and not in their actual draughtsmanship. Then there is Mr. H. M. Bateman, who works in a spirit of wild burlesque but has an amazingly clever technique; Mr. G. L. Stampa and Mr. George Belcher, both excellent observers of London types; Mr. Tom Webster, who is jester-in-chief to the world of sport and, like so many jesters, is really a shrewd commentator; the grave droll who signs himself "Fougasse"; and this is only to name the first that come to mind. There are no signs that the tradition of graphic humour is weakening in this present age. It is true that there is no single dominating genius, whose drawings will come to represent our age completely to posterity; and it may be that our own types are not being depicted with such truth and humour as may be found in the work of the 'seventies or 'nineties in the sketches of Keene or Phil May. On the other hand, there is certainly a great deal more variety in our comic art; and its humour, though it may be less robust, has a far wider application, is less frightened of ideas; and the best of it is free from those faults of taste, the vulgarity and obtuseness, that provoked Mrs. Meynell into condemning Victorian caricature. But always, to-day and yesterday, this graphic humour, in the hands of its masters, has been an indulgent criticism of life —satire, but satire tempered with affection and easy laughter; a small thing when compared with the mighty achievement of English comic literature, but being animated by and revealing the same spirit, as if it were so much appropriate decoration on that vast fabric, the native drollery shaping itself into gargoyles.

CHAPTER IV

A GALLOP AND A GOSSIP—I

THESE next two chapters will be nothing more (nor less) than a gallop through English literature and an accompanying gossip about its humour. Thus they will be severely limited. If any reader imagines that here, at last, justice will be done, that the roll of the humorists is about to be called, that the Recording Angel of humour will be present with his register, he is so grievously mistaken that he will be well advised to leave these chapters unread. We can only hope, at best, to pass in rapid and therefore defective survey the long pageant of English authors, and here and there, when we seem to hear laughter, stop to make an inquiry or two about the jest and jester. There will obviously be omissions by the score, and it will be impossible to make any comment whatever without outraging somebody's excellent taste. What is funny to one man is funereal to another, and for that there is no help. Yet we have all laughed in concert before now, and there has always been a stout majority ready to declare that Falstaff is an infinitely greater droll than Captain Bobadill. From these two little facts we may draw courage, at least, to begin.

We cannot do better than begin where so many of the text-books of literary history begin, with Chaucer. He was a poet and he was a humorist. Thus he is in truth the father of our literature, for poetry and humour are its two elements just as they were his. The range of Chaucer's humour is extraordinarily wide, from uproarious laughter at bawdy antics and horseplay to an irony so quiet, so delicate, that many readers never notice it is there at all or mistake it for naïveté. He had a huge zest for life, for people and things in the real world, for all the stir and bustle and movement of existence, for the variety in human action, motive, character. His sympathy was as broad as a shire. He had the truly æsthetic delight in whatever was full-blooded or high-spirited. Thus his gigantic comic portrait of the Wife of Bath glows with health and vitality, and is indeed something done once and for all: this wife of many husbands, who yet sighs for more, "meke and yonge, and fressh a-bed," is fit companion for Jack Falstaff himself. But for all Chaucer's zest for life and quick sympathies, there is always a part of him a little detached, ready to pounce on the least incongruity: and it is this mixture of qualities that makes him the great humorist he is. He laughs at us and he laughs at himself. It is characteristic of him that he should introduce himself into the company of pilgrims and then to us through the bantering remarks of the Host, that typical Englishman of the fourteenth century and any century since. The Host roars to the others to let this man have place:

> He in the waste is shapen as wel as I:
> This were a popet in an arme to enbrace
> For any woman, smal and faire of face.
> He seemeth elvish by his countenance,
> For unto no wight doth he dalliance.

(Somebody had once told Chaucer that he looked elvish; and the word fits the man.) And when he is fairly launched on his dreary Rime of Sir Thopas, he is stopped by the Host, who cries: "No more of this for Goddes dignitee!" And even in his tragic tales, Chaucer can never resist sly little jokes and touches of irony. A little tragedy goes a very long way with him: "No more of this!" he cries with one of his characters, and plunges zestfully into the comic view of life again. He was a great poet who was able to see himself as a droll figure, and there is nothing more rare in literature. Moreover, for all our talk of French Periods and Italian Periods, the man himself was as English as the beer that our Host supplied at his sign of the Tabard.

After Chaucer there is a wilderness, which, fortunately, we can cross at one bound. We arrive at the Elizabethans, whose humour is to be found in their drama. Shakespeare we must set aside, to be considered in another place, and once we have removed him and his great throng of comic figures there seems at first to be little left worth talking about. Comedy and buffoonery there are in plenty among these high-spirited dramatists, but somehow their humour does not haunt the memory as their melodrama or tragedy does: there is nobody as crazily comic as Webster and Tourneur are crazily tragic, and as we read these dramas again we are delighted a score of times by odd passages of great poetry for once that we are delighted by a sudden touch of humour. The weakness of the Elizabethan comic writing is that its action is usually improbable, grossly improbable, and—what is more important—

that its characters are mechanical "types" or merely personified humours and not droll individuals. And their authors, unlike Shakespeare, do not suffer these fools gladly; they give them any amount of space for buffoonery, but they do not seem to *enjoy* them as Shakespeare enjoyed his delightful fools. Not one of Ben Jonson's comic figures, for example, is in himself a gushing spring of folly; they are caricatures drawn in hard tight strokes, creatures of some arid desert of absurdity, monsters counterfeiting men for an evening. No doubt the rough bustle of *Bartholomew Fair* is funny enough on the stage, and there are moments of real humour—such as that when Sir Epicure Mammon tells Surly what he will do with his riches, in *The Alchemist*. But Bobadill in *Every Man in His Humour*, the cowardly swaggering captain, easily the most familiar comic figure in Elizabethan drama, is one of the few Jonson characters that achieve humour, and simply because his creator indulges him, gives him full scope for his folly. We see this in Bobadill's famous account of his plan for substituting the duello for general warfare:

I would select nineteen more, to myself, throughout the land; gentlemen they should be, of good spirit, strong, and able constitution; I would choose them by an instinct, a character that I have: and I would teach these nineteen, the special rules, as your punto, your reverso, your stoccata, your imbroccata, your passada, your montano; till they could all play very near, or altogether as well as myself. This done, say the enemy were forty thousand strong, we twenty

E

would come into the field, the tenth of March, or thereabouts; and we would challenge twenty of the enemy; they could not, in their honour, refuse us, well, we would kill them; challenge twenty more, kill them; twenty more, kill them; twenty more, kill them too; and thus, would we kill every man, his twenty a day, that's twenty score; twenty score, that's two hundred; two hundred a day, five days a thousand; forty thousand; forty times five, five times forty, two hundred days kills them all up, by cumputation. And this, will I venture my poor gentleman-like carcase to perform (provided there be no treason practised upon us) by fair, and discreet manhood, that is, civilly, by the sword.

Dekker, a gentler spirit, perhaps came nearer to humour than Ben did, with his Simon Eyre in *The Shoemaker's Holiday* and old Friscobaldo—a favourite of Hazlitt's—in the second part of *The Honest Whore*. And there is, of course, any amount of low comedy, rough bustling stuff, in Middleton, Heywood, and Massinger. But Beaumont and Fletcher, beginning a new tradition of comedy, are much better. In their *Wild Goose Chase, Monsieur Thomas, Rule a Wife and Have a Wife*, we have genuine high spirits that must be completely infectious in the theatre. Their delightful *Knight of the Burning Pestle* is the ancestor of a whole tribe of burlesques and farces. The Citizen and his wife, who insist upon a romantic play about a grocer, with their apprentice, Ralph, in the chief part, may have been introduced into the play for satirical purposes, but they are characters shrewdly and not unkindly observed in a spirit of humorous realism. Hear the goodwife when Ralph mounts the stage:

> I pray you, youth, let him have a suit of reparel! I'll be sworn, gentlemen, my husband tells you true: he will act you sometimes at our house, that all the neighbours cry out on him; he will fetch you up a couraging part so in the garret, that we are all as feared, I warrant you, that we quake again: we'll fear our children with him; if they never be so unruly, do but cry, "Ralph comes, Ralph comes!" to them, and they'll be as quiet as lambs. Hold up thy head, Ralph; show the gentlemen what thou canst do; speak a huffing part; I warrant you, the gentlemen will accept of it.

After Beaumont and Fletcher, the theatre falls into decay, and we will take leave of it for a little space, turning elsewhere while the Restoration wits polish their speeches behind the scenes.

Humour, as we have already seen, has been defined as "thinking in fun while feeling in earnest." The seventeenth century, from the outbreak of the Civil War onwards, is filled with writers who either thought in earnest and felt in earnest or thought in earnest and felt in fun—in short, with entirely serious authors, such as Milton, or with wits. Many of its best-known and most characteristic prose-writers, like Izaak Walton, Fuller, or Sir Thomas Browne, we think of as being "quaint," and we should be hard put to it to decide whether they had any real sense of humour or not. The Restoration brought the wits, and authorship became for the most part an affair of an inner knowing circle, composed of persons who had very few beliefs about anything and whose chief concern in life was to pass the time agreeably. The best of them had many accomplishments and must have made capital after-dinner companions, but some things they did not understand, and one of them was affection. They had no grasp upon the real world. Their minds were bright but brittle. They seem to be people of two dimensions instead of three, and a real man, such as Dryden, stands out among them like a being from another world. It was inevitable that wit should be their element and not humour. The age, however, gave us the man who is perhaps our greatest unconscious humorist—Pepys. And it certainly gave us some entertaining wits. One of the wildest and the shrewdest of them was Butler, the author of *Hudibras*, a long narrative poem that is a satire upon the Puritans and almost equally a satire upon opinion, religious, social, political, in general. The narrative itself is nothing; the manner of its recital, in which every device for startling us and making us laugh is used, and the author's very shrewd reflections, everything. Most of the tricks of comic rhymers of these last two hundred years may be found in Butler: the trick of using odd similes:

> And like a lobster boiled, the Morn
> From black to red began to turn;

the trick of grotesque rhyming:

> And straight another with his flambeau
> Gave Ralpho o'er the eyes a damn'd blow;

and so on and so forth. But in addition to these verbal buffooneries, which by themselves would only make the poem a companion to the *Ingoldsby Legends*, Butler gives us innumerable lines that have a cutting edge, thought so memorably expressed that though we never read him, we are for ever quoting him. It is not only the seventeenth-century Presbyterians who

> Compound for sins they are inclined to
> By damning those they have no mind to

or who are

> Still so perverse and opposite
> As if they worshipped God for spite.

Nor have any recent events proved that Butler was wrong when he remarked:

> He that complies against his will
> Is of the same opinion still.

It is surprising there has not been a re-discovery of Butler, now that his nonsense suits our nonsense.

We return to the theatre to find what is called the Artificial Comedy holding the stage. Congreve, Wycherley, Vanbrugh and Farquhar are its greatest practitioners. So much has been written about this school of dramatists that it would be absurd to let them take up much of our space here. What concerns us is their united contribution to English humour. Their weaknesses catch the eye at once. They present to us a world monstrously limited, made up, you might say, of a few chairs and a pasteboard tree or two, a world equally lacking in either ideas or affection, in which the men want nothing

but women and money, and the women want nothing
but men and fal-lals, in which you cannot imagine
birth or death or any event that could not be related
in the gossip column of a silly paper. Thus, they do
not make us feel that life itself is their quarry. These
wits have to be supplied with dummies, creatures
clearly labelled Fool, before they can show their wit
at all, and the thrusts they make may possibly have
worked havoc in St. James's Park in the year 1700
but now they no longer touch us at all. Lamb would
seem to have been right when he said of these plays
that "they are a world of themselves almost as much
as fairyland," that "the whole is a passing pageant,
where we should sit as unconcerned at the issues,
for life or death, as at a battle of the frogs and mice."
This, then, is their weakness, for your genuine
humorist of any size must throw his light upon life
as we know it. But it is also their strength, for once
we have agreed to escape with them from this real
world—as Lamb said he did, with pleasure—to take
a moral and philosophical holiday, then we find their
wit and absurd intrigues very entertaining. Perhaps
both the comic plotting and the character-drawing
have been equalled, if not bettered, by dramatists
before and since their time, but the dialogue of this
Comedy is the finest of its kind in English, seeming
absolutely natural, falling upon the ear like actual
speech, and yet closely packed with meaning and
character. Congreve, the best of them, has been over
praised as a wit pure and simple, but he can never
be over praised as a *writer* for the stage, a stylist.
He is—as Meredith remarked—at once precise and
voluble.

There are, of course, considerable differences between these four dramatists, who might be compared to liquors: Congreve is the finest dry champagne; Wycherley is full-bodied claret; Vanbrugh rather rough Burgundy; and Farquhar good old ale, that ale of which his Landlord Boniface declared: "'Tis smooth as oil, sweet as milk, clear as amber, and strong as brandy." There is nothing in English to equal the polish and brilliance of the dialogue in Congreve's *Way of the World*. Here it is at one extreme, in the enchanting airs and graces of Millamant, teasing her lover, Mirabel:

Millamant—Oh, I hate a lover that can dare to think he draws a moment's air, independent of the bounty of his mistress. There is not so impudent a thing in nature, as the saucy look of an assured man, confident of success. The pedantic arrogance of a very husband has not so pragmatical an air. Ah! I'll never marry, unless I am first made sure of my will and pleasure.

Mirabel—Would you have 'em both before marriage? Or will you be contented with the first now, and stay for the other till after grace?

Millamant—Ah! don't be impertinent. My dear liberty, shall I leave thee? my faithful solitude, my darling contemplation, must I bid you then adieu? Ay-h adieu—my morning thoughts, agreeable wakings, indolent slumbers, all ye *douceurs*, ye *sommeils du matin*, adieu? I can't do't, 'tis more than impossible—positively, Mirabel, I'll lie abed in a morning as long as I please.

Mirabel—Then I'll get up in a morning as early as I please.

Millamant—Ah! idle creature, get up when you will, and d'ye hear, I won't be called names after I'm married; positively I won't be called names.

Mirabel—Names!

Millamant—Ay, as wife, spouse, my dear, joy, jewel, love, sweetheart, and the rest of the nauseous cant, in which men and their wives are so fulsomely familiar—I shall never bear that— good Mirabel, don't let us be familiar or fond, nor kiss before folks, like my Lady Fadler and Sir Francis; nor go to Hyde Park together the first Sunday in a new chariot, to provoke eyes and whispers, and then never to be seen together again; as if we were proud of one another the first week, and ashamed of one another ever after. Let us never visit together, nor go to a play together; but let us be very strange and well bred; let us be strange as if we had been married a great while; and as well bred as if we were not married at all.

And here it is at the other extreme, with Lady Wishfort scolding her woman, Foible:

Lady Wishfort—Out of my house, out of my house, thou viper! thou serpent, that I have fostered! thou bosom traitress, that I have raised from nothing! Begone! begone! begone! Go! go! That I took from washing of old gauze and weaving of dead hair, with a bleak blue nose over a chafing-dish of starved embers, and dining behind a traverse rag, in a shop no bigger than a birdcage! Go, go! starve again, do, do!

Foible—Dear madam, I'll beg pardon on my knees.

Lady Wishfort—Away! out! out! Go, set up for yourself again! Do, drive a trade, do, with your threepennyworth of small ware, flaunting upon a packthread, under a brandy-seller's bulk, or against a dead wall by a ballad-monger! Go, hang out an old Frisoneer gorget, with a yard of yellow colberteen again. Do; an old gnawed mask, two rows of pins, and a child's fiddle; a glass necklace with the beads broken, and a quilted nightcap with one ear. Go, go, drive a trade! These were your commodities, you treacherous trull! this was the merchandise you dealt in when I took you into my house, placed you next myself, and made you governante of my whole family! You have forgot this, have you, now you have feathered your nest?

Wycherley never achieved the grace of the one nor the fury of the other. His comedies are more solidly constructed than Congreve's, very vigorous masculine affairs, and so fit the stage better, in spite of their coarseness, which becomes at times a sickening nastiness. They are filled with bold character-drawing, but Wycherley's rough satirical temper keeps him from humour proper: his people are too violently presented to be really funny, at least in the library. Hazlitt sadly over-praises him. There is more genuine humour in Vanbrugh, whose comedies have not the weight of Wycherley's but have infinitely more verve and warmth. His gay indecencies are a very different matter from Wycherley's cold coarseness. There is a fine bustle in the intrigues of

The Relapse and *The Confederacy*, and a real sense of comic character. His Lord Foppington is the best of all the fashionable dandies in these comedies: his account of the way in which he spends his time, to Amanda, who mentions reading, is excellent fooling:

> That, I must confess, I am not altogether so fond of. Far to my mind, the inside of a book, is to entertain one's self with the forc'd product of another man's brain. Naw I think a man of quality and breeding may be much diverted with the natural sprauts of his own. But to say the truth, madam, let a man love reading never so well, when once he comes to know this tawn, he finds so many better ways of passing away the four-and-twenty hours, that 'twere ten thousand pities he shou'd consume his time in that."

Farquhar, the last of this school of dramatists, brings something new with him, the open air and youthful high spirits. In his two best pieces, *The Recruiting Officer*, which was played throughout the century and was the first play ever to be acted in Australia, where convicts performed it at Sydney in 1789, and *The Beaux' Stratagem*, which has recently been revived with considerable success, we escape from the town into the country and real open air. (The famous ditty, "Over the hills and far away," is from *The Recruiting Officer*.) His dialogue may have less wit and fine writing in it than that of his brother dramatists, but it has even more character and energy. Hear Mrs. Sullen, in *The Beaux' Stratagem*, complaining of her brutish husband:

"O sister, sister! If ever you marry, beware of a sullen, silent sot, one that's always musing, but never thinks. There's some diversion in a talking blockhead; and since a woman must wear chains, I would have the pleasure of hearing 'em rattle a little. Now you shall see—but take this by the way: he came home this morning, at his usual hour of four, wakened me out of a sweet dream of something else, by tumbling over the tea-table, which he broke all to pieces; after his man and he had rolled about the room, like sick passengers in a storm, he comes flounce into bed, dead as a salmon into a fishmonger's basket; his feet cold as ice, his breath hot as a furnace, and his hands and his face as greasy as his flannel nightcap. O matrimony! He tosses up the clothes with a barbarous swing over his shoulders, disorders the whole economy of my bed, leaves me half naked, and my whole night's comfort is the tuneable serenade of that wakeful nightingale, his nose! Oh, the pleasure of counting the melancholy clock by a snoring husband!"

On a different level, but equally good, is the report of Scrub, the oafish servant in the same play, after he has been sent by his mistress to gather information concerning the stranger seen in church:

Dorinda—Well, Scrub, what news of the gentleman?

Scrub—Madam, I have brought you a packet of news.

Dorinda—Open it quickly, come.

Scrub—In the first place I inquired who the gentleman was; they told me he was a stranger.

Secondly, I asked what the gentleman was; they answered and said, that they never saw him before. Thirdly, I inquired what countryman he was; they replied, 'twas more than they knew. Fourthly, I demanded whence he came; their answer was, they could not tell. And fifthly, I asked whither he went; and they replied, they knew nothing of the matter, and this is all I could learn.

We have all met Scrub in our time, and we can do worse than take our leave of these dramatists with a mention of him.

Swift was born in Ireland and died there, but, nevertheless, he was an Englishman and so can claim a place here. But what sort of place he should be given here is not easy to determine. He is undoubtedly one of the great ironists of the world, but how stands his account with Humour? Humour is there, but it is not the air and body of him; you merely catch glimpses of it in his work as you might catch the flashes of a sword waved in the sunlight. There is pity and there is affection in the finest humour; and even when you step lower down, you find indulgence at least. The terrible Dean could regard his fellow creatures—if we except a few intimates—with neither affection nor indulgence; he made no allowances, gave no quarter; he loathed the species to which he belonged. Thackeray brought him into his *English Humourists* only to turn him into a Richard Crookback and a Timon combined and magnified, a monstrous figure of darkness; all of which, no doubt, came of seeing the Dean against a background that was not his, in the gentle company of the true humorists. It would be better to leave him out altogether. Yet it is difficult to do that. Think of the *Tale of a Tub*, or *Gulliver*, now, by an irony richer than our author's, a standing dish for the nursery. Is there not humour in the grave details of Gulliver's life among the pygmies and the giants, his pocketing the Lilliputian courtier and his sedan chair, the hanging of his boat to dry in Brobdingnag? And there is fun—more than most critics seem willing to allow—in the wild schemes and customs of Laputa. But Swift's humour best displays itself in his occasional pieces, such as the *Directions to Servants* and the very funny, if rather cruel, bantering of the prophetic Partridge, whose death was predicted by Swift in his burlesque and then solemnly announced later and insisted upon, in spite of the protests of the unhappy astrologer. There is humour, too, if of a rather grim sort, in some of the Dean's verses, such as those lines on his own death:

See, how the dean begins to break!
Poor gentleman! he droops apace!
You plainly find it in his face.
That old vertigo in his head
Will never leave him till he's dead.
Besides his memory decays:
He recollects not what he says;
He cannot call his friends to mind;
Forgets the place where he has dined;
Plies you with stories o'er and o'er—
  He told them fifty times before.
  How does he fancy we can sit
  To hear his out-of-fashion wit?

It was a tip from Swift, who threw out a suggestion for a Newgate pastoral, that helped his friend Gay to find a little easy-chair among the humorists. Gay, who had written some light verse whose charm still survives, developed this suggestion into the ever-delightful *Beggar's Opera*, in which both the lyrics, full of graceful absurdities, and the deft witty dialogue could not be bettered.

English humour takes a new turn with the arrival of the *Tatler* and the *Spectator*. In the work of the periodical essayists we find neither hard wit nor buffoonery, but an easy, gentle flow of true humour. Nobody will pretend that Sir Roger de Coverley, Will Wimble, Will Honeycomb, and the rest are comic figures of any great stature, the equal of Falstaff or Uncle Toby or Mr. Micawber. Neither Addison nor Steele (who has no right to be here, being an Irishman, but we cannot separate the two now) was a creator, a comic genius; they were both commentators, sketching smilingly their age. Humour such as theirs is like a little shower of rain; it comes and goes lightly, but everything is the greener and fresher for it. Steele alone, perhaps, could be described as a humorist proper; he was—as Hazlitt remarks—a less artificial and more original writer: "The humorous descriptions of Steele resemble loose sketches, or fragments of a comedy; those of Addison are rather comments, or ingenious paraphrases, on the genuine text." Addison's observations on cheerfulness well illustrate his character:

I have always preferred cheerfulness to mirth. The latter I consider as an act, the former as an habit of the mind. Mirth is short and transient, cheerfulness fixed and permanent. Those are often raised into the greatest transports of mirth who are subject to the greatest depression of melancholy: on the contrary, cheerfulness, though it does not give the mind such an exquisite gladness, prevents us from falling into any depths of sorrow. Mirth is like a flash of lightning that breaks through a gloom of clouds, and glitters for a moment; cheerfulness keeps up a kind of daylight in the mind, and fills it with a steady and perpetual serenity.

It is a pleasant safe view of things and it certainly never yet turned a man into a great humorist. Steele had a very different disposition: he laughed and cried at life, and though he was not the writer his friend was, though he wrote with the printer's boy waiting in one corner and his boon companions waiting in another, he can move us to laughter and tears with him at life two centuries after he has done with it. These two essayists (Steele more especially) should be praised for bringing back affection into humour. They could like or love and still laugh. Their best papers banish the wit's contempt for a fool and give humour that easy playful domestic turn which is so characteristically English. They smile at the world in an atmosphere of firelight and friendliness. If we wish to realize the nature and scope of their achievement, what it was they brought into the literature of their time, we have only to imagine what Congreve or Wycherley would have made of Sir Roger and his widow. The vast popularity of these two essayists outlived their century. Not a few boys, themselves novelists and essayists in after life, counted the *Tatler* and *Spectator* among the first friends they made in the family library. Their influence can hardly be over estimated, and it was as good and welcome as a bright fire in December. It helped to warm our humour.

We have now reached the age of satire, of pungent or graceful wit, of unabashed scurrility, of the exquisite Pope and graceful Prior at the beginning of the century, or rough rhymers like Churchill and "Peter Pindar" at its middle and towards its close, and of epigrammatists in shoals. All these we must deny ourselves. So, too, we have no time to spare for the many delightful letter-writers, Lady Mary Wortley Montagu, Horace Walpole, Gray, Cowper and the rest, most of whom are either wits or masters of a sprightly fancy but none of whom can strictly be considered humorists.

The eighteenth-century novel yields, on the whole, but a poor return of humour. The exceptions are very great indeed—Fielding and Sterne take their place in any company, but they will be dealt with in a later chapter. Nor is the drama any better, from our point of view. To begin with, the two out-standing comic dramatists, Sheridan and Goldsmith, were both Irishmen, and so was Macklin, perhaps the best of those that remain. Foote has already had his share of our attention. The elder Colman con-trived a few passable comic figures. Both Mrs. Inchbald and Thomas Holcroft had an excellent sense of the theatre, but they do not give us any humour worth discussing. As those old volumes of collected plays, tightly packed in double columns, the *British Theatre*, the *London Stage*, and so forth, amply testify, this century was extraordinarily prolific in the theatre, producing any number of comedies, farces, ballad operas, burlesques that were still thought to be worth printing fifty years after they first appeared. We can recognize these things at a glance: the characters in high life always bear such names as *Sir Simon Flourish*, *Captain Sightly*, *Lady Vibrate*, *Don Carlos de Pimentel*, *Miss La Blond*; and the characters in low life are always called *Tug*, *Snare*, *Bundle*, *Scrip*, *Hodge*, *Peggy*, and *Dame Paddock*; and nine times out of ten the plot turns on a rich uncle and a poor nephew, a clandestine courtship and an elopement, and the fun has to be found in a few dialogues at cross-purposes, a silly old man or a fop and a stupid country servant. Probably a very large number of good acting comedies and farces can be found in this eighteenth-century drama, but they are mostly poor things to read, and as we have never seen them quickened into life in the theatre, we must let them go.

"He was the most humorous man I ever knew." This was Sir John Hawkins' opinion of Dr. Johnson. We should never think of including him as a writer among the English humorists. There have been few authors more weighty and grave. His creative works, such as *The Vanity of Human Wishes*, *Irene*, and *Rasselas*, are filled with what he himself would call "inspissated gloom." His periodical essays, especially those in The *Rambler*, achieve unconscious humour in their ponderous efforts to be sprightly. The papers of The *Idler* are generally lighter in tone, and some of the character sketches, of Dick Minim,

F

Jack Whirler, and the rest, have a genuine drollery.
Once we have left Johnson the writer for Johnson
the talker, the man we meet in the records of Boswell
and Mrs. Piozzi, we can no longer be surprised at
Hawkins' verdict. It is hardly necessary at this date
to sketch his character. He knew a great deal about
life and did not think much of it. He had a deep-
seated melancholy (the old black dog that has
followed so many great humorists) that never left
him except when he was in good company. In
Boswell's book, we see him, in Professor Gordon's
fine phrase, "after the storms of life, like a man-of-
war in harbour receiving visitors." The genial
excitement of talk drives away all gloomy thoughts of
the misery of men's lives in this world and the mystery
of their entry into the next, and we discover Johnson
pugnacious and gay and sometimes altogether given
up to nonsense and a "frolick." Boswell is apt to
pass quickly over these latter moods:

"I passed many hours with him on the 17th, of
which I find all my memorial is, "much laughing."
It should seem he had that day been in a humour
for jocularity and merriment, and upon such
occasions I never knew a man laugh more
heartily. We may suppose, that the high relish
of a state so different from his habitual gloom,
produced more than ordinary exertions of that
distinguishing faculty of man, which has puzzled
philosophers so much to explain. . . .

And there can be doubt that Jowett was right when
he suggested that Boswell quite unconsciously

tended to misrepresent his hero by throwing the emphasis upon the grave sage and philosopher and keeping in the background the boon companion, the man who, when knocked up at three in the morning by his young friends, Beauclerk and Langton, cried: "What, is it you, you dogs? I'll have a frisk with you," and promptly did have a frisk with them. Even a Johnson finds it difficult to be at his lightest and easiest in the presence of a hero-worshipper, taking notes. Nevertheless we have a share in his fun and nonsense. But his humour is something more than that, and the spirit of it pervades nearly all the best talk in the book. It comes from the mingling in him of many different strains, his deep affection and tenderness, his pugnacity, his tolerance for persons and intolerance for ideas, the play of prejudice over the depths of his sagacity. And there is always something humorous, too, in *character* itself, its assembly of habits, tastes, whims, and for massive bulk of character you can hardly better Johnson. Once more we return to that definition of humour which we have touched on several times, the "thinking in fun while feeling in earnest." It fits Johnson like a glove, for his feelings were always deep and steady, but he was rarely solemn in his thinking, having none of that veneration for ideas which we find in philosophical doctrinaires. Nobody is more English than Dr. Johnson. He remains one of our greatest figures, and it would have been strange if he had not been, among other things, a humorist.

CHAPTER V

A GALLOP AND A GOSSIP—II

WE arrive at the age of the Romantics. Here there are more people, it seems, without any sense of humour at all, but on the other hand, when humour does break in, it is discovered to be better than it was before. Romance brings in not only the solemn Wordsworth and the passionate Shelley— both of them without humour—but such a one as Lamb, with his grave, wild jesting, on which there also falls that light that never was on land or sea. (But Lamb deserves a chapter to himself, and shall have one.) Meanwhile, no sooner had the Romantics sounded a note or two than up popped the parodists, and burlesque took a new turn. A few score literary historians are ready to explain that Canning and his young friends of *The Anti-Jacobin* were political satirists, and so, indeed, they were, but undoubtedly they were also a number of high-spirited young gentlemen out for a lark. That is why their parodies have lasted so long: they are gloriously absurd. We can still enjoy:

"I give thee sixpence! I will see thee damn'd first.
Wretch! whom no sense of wrongs can rouse to vengeance
Sordid, unfeeling, reprobate, degraded spiritless outcast!"

(*Kicks the knife-grinder, overturns his wheel, and exit in a transport of republican enthusiasm and universal philanthropy.*)

or the burlesque of *The Rovers*, with its highfalutin soliloquies, its songs:

> There, first for thee my passion grew,
> Sweet! sweet Matilda Pottingen!
> Thou wast the daughter of my Tu-
> -tor, *Law Professor* at the U-
> -niversity of Gottingen!
> -niversity of Gottingen!

Its astonishing stage directions:

> Several soldiers cross the stage wearily, as if returning from the Thirty Years' War.

There is nothing so riotous in the *Rejected Addresses* of James and Horace Smith, who are more sober parodists and have perhaps been rather over-praised, though such things as James Smith's parody of Crabbe:

> John Richard William Alexander Dwyer,
> Was footman to Justinian Stubbs, Esquire,
> But when John Dwyer 'listed in the Blues,
> Emmanuel Jennings polished Stubbs's shoes.
> Emmanuel Jennings brought his youngest boy
> Up as a corn-cutter, a safe employ. . . .

could hardly be improved. There is no need to trace the history of parody down the century. The honours in prose fall to Thackeray, with his delightful burlesque novels, and to Mr. Max Beerbohm, whose *Christmas Garland* contains the most devastating and yet most subtle imitations (and, indirectly, criticisms) of the matter and manner of well-known authors that we have in English. The honours in verse must be widely distributed among C. S. Calverley, J. K. Stephen, Sir Owen Seaman and Mr. J. C. Squire, though it must not be forgotten that Swinburne himself—a favourite though never really an easy victim of the parodists—produced some amazingly good examples of the art, a little art that time seems to have looked upon with favour.

The Regency—to which we must now return—was a time of wits and jokers, when men could dine out nightly on puns and impromptus. We catch many an echo of this crackle of laughter round the dinner-tables in the memoirs of the period. The greatest of these wits was Sydney Smith. His works, though largely reviews and pamphlets, can still be read with pleasure, for they are luminous with good sense and at times really funny; but it is obvious that they are only a shadow of the man himself, whose comicality could not be resisted by any sort of company, from the rustic servants at Foston to Lord and Lady Holland. (He could be sharp even with that imperious great lady. "Sydney," she once commanded, "ring the bell." "And shall I sweep the room?" he inquired.) We will not break into the immense store of witty anecdotes that have gathered about his name and memory; the best are too well-known and the others do not matter. Sydney Smith was certainly the greatest of the Regency dinner-table humorists, perhaps because he was something more than a mere society entertainer. A lower order of wits is well represented by Theodore Hook, popular for a time as a novelist (and not without influence upon young Boz) and really famous as a practical joker and *improvisatore*. Perhaps the best thing recorded of him is the verse he made when once interrupted in a song at the piano by the arrival of one Winter, a tax-collector:

Here comes Mr. Winter, collector of taxes;
I'd advise you to pay him whatever he axes;
Excuses won't do; he stands no sort of flummery,
Though Winter his name is, his process is summary.

The first of the novelists worth considering is Peacock, who is, indeed, nine-tenths pure humour. He is frequently described as a satirist, but this gives a wrong idea of both his aims and his achievements. All his strange tales contain satire—one of them, the weakest, *Melincourt*, contains a great deal—but he had really no other object in writing them than to laugh at the world. He was not a reformer, or a moralist, or even a cynic, though there is a kind of ripe disillusionment behind his bland irony. What makes him a unique figure is that he is a humorist who chooses to play with ideas and with hardly anything else. He brings fun into the high and dry atmosphere of exposition and debate. His favourite butts are philosophical enthusiasts, especially those who believe that one thing alone will save the world. He fastens upon the cranks. And yet it cannot be said that he makes himself the spokesman of common sense, of the ordinary man, for obviously he likes ideas and philosophical enthusiasts, and even cranks, so long as they are genial cranks. His novels create a little world of their own, in which nobody does anything but eat and drink and talk and occasionally travel and make love. Talk is the action in these novels. We spend most of our time in them sitting round a well-stocked table, listening to rather absurd and unlikely people arguing with tremendous gusto. They never convince one another, these people of his, but they talk away, pass the bottle, sing a song or two, and are as happy as any people we ever met in or out of fiction. All this is amusing enough, but Peacock would not occupy the position he does if it were not for his superb style, which is precise and finely turned and yet saturated with wit and humour. To begin quoting from such delightful things as *Nightmare Abbey* and *Crotchet Castle*, his two best novels, of talk, would be fatal, for we should have to go on throughout the rest of the chapter; but we can spare a little space for a passage or two from *The Misfortunes of Elphin*, which is his best tale—a little masterpiece of genial irony—and is singularly undervalued. It is there we meet Prince Seithenyn, the best comic toper outside Shakespeare, and a master of strangely fuddled logic. What an astonishing speech is that in which he defends his policy of doing nothing to the embankment in his charge! He admits that it is decayed, but remains unruffled:

Decay is one thing, and danger is another. Everything that is old must decay. That the embankment is old, I am free to confess; that it is somewhat rotten in parts, I will not altogether deny; that it is any the worse for that, I do most sturdily gainsay. It does its business well; it works well; it keeps out the water from the land; and it lets in the wine upon the High Commissioner of Embankment. Cupbearer, fill. Our ancestors were wiser than we: they built it in their wisdom: and, if we should be so rash as to try to mend it, we should only mar it. . . .

That some parts of it are rotten does not trouble him at all: he has his exquisite reasons:

But I say, the parts that are rotten give elasticity to those that are sound: they give them elasticity, elasticity, elasticity. If it were all sound, it would break by its own obstinate stiffness: the soundness is checked by the rottenness, and the stiffness is balanced by the elasticity.

And what a reeling ripe logic there is in his denial of his own death, when he turns up again after being missing for twenty years:

"Seithenyn," said Taliesin, "has slept twenty years under the waters of the western sea, as King Gwythno's *Lamentations* have made known to all Britain."

"They have not made it known to me," said Seithenyn, "for the best of all reasons, that one can only know the truth: for, if that which we think we know is not truth, it is something we do not know. A man cannot know his own death; for, while he knows anything, he is alive; at least, I never heard of a dead man who knew anything, or pretended to know anything; if he had so pretended, I should have told him to his face he was no dead man. . . ."

This does not give any idea of Peacock in his favourite part, as the comedian of ideas, or "the laughing philosopher," but it is a good specimen of his original and altogether delightful humour. That humour finds its way into verse as well as prose, as the various songs in the novels testify. There is nothing better of its kind in English than the *War Song of Dinas Vawr*:

> The mountain sheep are sweeter,
> But the valley sheep are fatter;
>   We, therefore, deemed it meeter
>   To carry off the latter.
> We made an expedition;
> We met a host, and quelled it;
> We forced a strong position,
>   And killed the men who held it.

Peacock's best work is now a century old, yet his reputation is steadily growing. His sophisticated ironic humour—like a dry old sherry—will never be to everybody's taste, but more and more readers are discovering in this relatively obscure eccentric author a genuine, a unique humorist.

If we wanted to find a contrast to Peacock's humour, so clipped and scholarly, we could find it in Marryat or Surtees. Marryat carries on the tradition of high jinks that began with Smollett, who has not been noticed here because, like some other professors of high jinks, such as Charles Lever and Michael Scott, he was not English. These stories of life in the army or navy, stories in which the heroes were always either fighting the French or their brother officers, drinking port and brandy, and eating devilled

kidneys, making very perfunctory love and playing very elaborate practical jokes, were very
popular. Marryat, however, is above the average
both as a storyteller and a humorist. There is a good
deal of knock-about fun in his work, but there is,
too, some genuine humour. Mr. Easy, that domestic
philosopher, with his theory of names and his system
of rectifying the mistakes of nature by compressing
and enlarging men's bumps, is capital fun. Mr.
Chucks, the genteel 'bosun, is even better. He, too,
is an authority upon names:

"No name can be too fine for a pretty girl, or a
good frigate, Mr. Simple; for my part, I'm very
fond of these hard names. Your Bess, and Poll,
and Sue, do very well for the Point, or Castle Rag;
but in my opinion they degrade a lady. Don't
you observe, Mr. Simple, that all our gunbrigs,
a sort of vessel that will certainly d—n the inventor
to all eternity, have nothing but low, common
names, such as Pincher, Thrasher, Boxer, Badger,
and all that sort, which are quite good enough for
them; whereas all our dashing, saucy frigates have
names as long as the maintop bowling, and hard
enough to break your jaw—such as Melpomeny,
Terpsichory, Arethusy, Bacchanty—fine flourishes,
as long as their pennants which dip alongside in
a calm."

"Very true," replied I; "but do you think, then,
that it is the same with family names?'

"Most certainly, Mr. Simple, When I was in
good society, I rarely fell in with such names as
Potts, or Bell, or Smith, or Hodges; it was always

Mr. Fortesque, or Mr. FitzGerald, or Mr. Fitz-
Herbert; seldom bowed, sir, to anything under
three syllables.'

"Then I presume, Mr. Chucks, you are not fond
of your own name?"

'There you touch me, Mr. Simple; but it is
quite good enough for a boatswain,' replied Mr.
Chucks with a sigh."

It is probably Surtees' horses and hounds rather
than his jokes that have made him so popular with
one section of the public, a class that does more
riding than reading. His first book, *Jorrocks' Jaunts
and Jollities*, is of some interest because it represents
what *Pickwick Papers* was originally intended to be,
and would have been if Dickens had not been a man
of genius. Jorrocks himself is a character sketched
with a certain comic gusto, but in this first book
neither he nor his adventures seem quite credible.
He is much better in *Handley Cross*, which is altogether a better piece of work. James Pigg is admirable, and perhaps the best thing in the book is his
famous remark when he and Jorrocks have been
holding forth over the bottle:

The fire began to hiss, and Mr. Jorrocks felt
confident his prophecy was about to be fulfilled.
"Look out of the winder, James, and see wot-un
a night it is," said he to Pigg, giving the log a stir,
to ascertain that the hiss didn't proceed from any
dampness in the wood.

James staggered up, and after a momentary
grope about the room—for they were sitting

without candles—exclaimed: "Hellish dark, and smells of cheese!"

"Smells o' cheese!" repeated Mr. Jorrocks, looking round in astonishment; "smells o' cheese! —vy, man, you've got your nob i' the cupboard— this be the vinder!"

There is, too, some good fantastic fooling in that scene with the little old fox-hunter who, at breakfast, suddenly hurls his cup out of the window and claps the saucer on his head. The horses and hounds, the loud hallooing, the real sense of open air and movement in these sketchy tales, carry off the author's crudities, vulgarities, and repetitions, and make it possible even for those of us who are not sportsmen to find some pleasure in the antics of Jorrocks and his friends. Nevertheless, to imagine—as some people appear to do—that Jorrocks is one of our major comic characters, fit company for Falstaff and Parson Adams and Uncle Toby and Mr. Micawber, is entirely absurd.

This was the time when comic verse became so popular. We think at once of *The Ingoldsby Legends*, which our grandfathers knew by heart. It cannot be said that their author, Barham, had much real humour, nor was he exactly a wit. He had a taste, which his contemporaries shared, for the comic gruesome, a kind of fun that has lost its appeal and, no doubt, even repels a great many readers, who feel more inclined to shudder than to laugh when they arrive at such a legend as that of *The Knight and the Lady*:

Oh! 'tis shocking to view
The sight which the corpse reveals!

Sir Thomas's body, it looks so odd—he
  Was half eaten up by the eels!
His waistcoat and hose, and the rest of his clothes
Were all gnawed through and through;
And out of each shoe an eel they drew;
And from each of his pockets they pull'd out two.
And the Gardener himself had secreted a few,
  As well we may suppose;
For, when he came running to give the alarm,
He had six in the basket that hung on his arm. . . .

With the fair widow's remark as a climax:

Eels a many I've ate; but any
So good ne'er tasted before!
They're a fish, too, of which I'm remarkably fond,
Go—pop Sir Thomas again in the pond,
Poor dear!—HE'LL CATCH US SOME MORE! !

The jest is there, but, like the eels, it demands a
strong stomach to be relished at all. Side by side
with this taste for the comic gruesome—indeed,
frequently overlapping it—was a taste for the comic
grotesque, for spectres and witches, bloody-head-
and-raw-bones fun, a taste that Barham exploits at
length. Where he succeeds it is by virtue of his
tremendous energy and gusto in rhyming rather than
by any merit in his powers of comic invention. He
jingles and jangles you into sharing his high spirits:

There's a cry and a shout, and a deuce of a rout,
And nobody seems to know what they're about,
But the monks have their pockets all turned
  inside out;

The friars are kneeling, and hunting and feeling
The carpet, the floor, and the walls, and the ceiling.
The Cardinal drew off each plum-coloured shoe,
And left his red stockings exposed to the view;
He peeps, and he feels in the toes and the heels;
They turn up the dishes—they turn up the plates,
They take up the poker and poke out the grates,
They turn up the rugs, they examine the mugs:
But no! no such thing; they can't find THE RING!
And the Abbot declared that, "when nobody
    twigg'd it,
Some rascal or other had popp'd in, and prigg'd it!"

There are times, however, when his comicality can
become very grim indeed and have a cutting edge
to it, as in that "Sporting Anecdote" of Lord Tom-
noddy and his friends, who stayed up all night at the
"Magpie and Stump" to see the execution, and were
then unlucky enough to fall asleep over their liquor
and so "miss all the fun."

Hood comes next. He, too, had a taste for the comic
gruesome, as we discover in such things as *Mary's
Ghost*:

The arm that used to take your arm,
    Is took to Dr. Vyse;
And both my legs are gone to walk
    The hospital at Guy's.
I vow'd that you should have my hand
    But fate gives us denial;
You'll find it there, at Dr. Bell's,
    In spirits and a phial. . . .

But Hood happened to be a real poet, and his
jesting has a different air from that of most of his

contemporaries. He had—as he declared in his own whimsical, half melancholy fashion—to be "a lively Hood for a livelihood." There is about him a suggestion of one of Shakespeare's Fools, who grin and snap their bony fingers and reel off their puns while Death is darkening the sky above their heads. There is something desperate about his punning humour, and we know that it is only a step from such things as *Faithless Nelly Gray*:

> Ben Battle was a soldier bold,
>   And used to war's alarms:
> But a cannon-ball took off his legs,
>   So he laid down his arms!
> Now as they bore him off the field,
>   Said he, "Let others shoot,
> For here I leave my second leg,
>   And the Forty-second Foot!"

to the *Song of the Shirt* and the *Bridge of Sighs*. His *Miss Kilmansegg*, though full of grotesquely comic lines, is really a satire, and is, indeed, one of the best satirical poems of the century. And after Hood comes Praed, whose charming light verse can hardly be discussed as humorous literature, but whose choicest things—such as *The Vicar* and *Quince*—are, in Austin Dobson's words, "rather humorous character-painting of a very delicate and individual kind than absolute *vers de société*." Who does not remember the Vicar:

> His talk was like a spring, which runs
>   With rapid change from rocks to roses:

It slipped from politics to puns,
  It passed from Mohamet to Moses;
Beginning with the laws which keep
  The planets in their radiant courses,
And ending with some precept deep
  For dressing eels, or shoeing horses.

He was a shrewd and sound Divine,
  Of loud Dissent the mortal terror;
And when, by dint of page and line,
  He 'stablished Truth, or startled Error,
The Baptist found him far too deep;
  The Deist sighed with saving sorrow;
And the lean Levite went to sleep,
  And dreamed of tasting pork to-morrow. . . .

There is sufficient body in such verses as these to
admit their author into the ranks of the humorists.
We are now in the middle of the Victorian Age,
and are, if you will, in a wilderness of horsehair and
antimacassars, and dark gas-lit houses and the Great
Exhibition, and *The Idylls of the King* and Frith's
Derby Day, and bad oratorio and monster quadrilles,
and *Good Words* and *Eric, or Little by Little*, and whatever else the patient malice of our newest historians
and biographers may disclose. But—oddly enough
—we are also in an age when English humour was
extraordinarily rich and fertile. The most sparkling
and refreshing springs of fun come gushing out of
this wilderness. Thus, Mr. Chesterton can declare:
"Of the Victorian Age as a whole it is true to say
that it did discover a new thing: a thing called
Nonsense." They discovered it and they revelled
in it. The nonsense that these Victorians first

G

brought into the light is—as a recent foreign critic, M. Cammaerts, has admitted—a specifically English contribution to the world's literature. It combines, in a new way, those two essential English literary qualities, poetry and humour. It is unreason triumphant. It is absurdity carried into a poetical atmosphere. It is a happy holiday away from the world of sense, a glimpse of another and even madder world than this. The strongest and sanest minds have always delighted in it, as much as if not more than the children for whom it is frequently supposed to be produced. It is one of the kingdoms of Romance. The best nonsense of Edward Lear seems just as inspired as the best poetry of Coleridge. We feel that we could no more achieve the Dong with the Luminous Nose merely by taking thought than we could achieve *Kubla Khan*. Lear gives us the high fantastical of the absurd. He is the laureate of some blue moon. When we read *The Jumblies*:

> They went to sea in a Sieve, they did,
>   In a Sieve they went to sea:
> In spite of all their friends could say
> On a winter's morn, on a stormy day
>   In a Sieve they went to sea!

with its strangely mournful refrain:

> Far and few, far and few,
> Are the lands where the Jumblies live;
> Their heads are green, and their hands are blue,
>   And they went to sea in a Sieve.

or the story of the *Courtship of the Yonghy-Bonghy-Bo*:

On the coast of Coromandel
Where the early pumpkins blow,
In the middle of the woods
Lived the Yonghy-Bonghy-Bo.
Two old chairs, and half a candle,
One old jug without a handle,
   These were all his wordly goods:
   In the middle of the woods,
   These were all the wordly goods,
Of the Yonghy-Bonghy-Bo,
Of the Yonghy-Bonghy-Bo.

We feel that we are reading the perfectly serious narrative verse of some distant and crazy planet, where may be found oblong oysters and runcible hats and bottles of Ring-Bo-Ree, and Ploffskin, Pluffskin, Pelican jee, the sunset isles of Boshen, and the hills of the Chankly Bore. Here, too, are all the strange people of the limericks, the old man in the tree who was horribly bored by a bee, the old man of Jamaica who suddenly married a Quaker, the old man who ran up and down in his grandmother's gown, the old person of Anerley who rushed down the Strand with a peg in each hand, and many another, all doing the last thing that one would expect them to do. With Lear we reach Ultima Thule.

By his side we must, of course, put Lewis Carroll, who achieves a kind of nonsense not so wildly romantic as Lear's, but equally delightful. Indeed, when we consider his achievement, the two *Alice* stories, the *Hunting of the Snark,* and all the other odds and ends of nonsense (including at least a chapter or two from *Sylvie and Bruno*), we must acknowledge his supreme mastery of this strange craft. There may be heights of craziness, on which Lear is perched, crooning his little songs, that Lewis Carroll never reached, but on the other hand his is the most sustained nonsense we have and the most piquant. Not only has he given us nonsensical verse (and even Lear, perhaps, has nothing richer and wilder than *Jabberwocky*), but he has also given us the prose fiction of nonsense, created for us a whole daft world. What is so wonderful in the two *Alice* books is the combination of the genuine dream atmosphere and a kind of insane logic. Half the characters seem to be mad metaphysicians. They seem to argue reasonably enough and yet all their conclusions are moonshine. The world that Alice visits (for Wonderland and the Looking-Glass country are obviously neighbouring territories) is as puzzling and droll as some distant planet would be, but it seems consistent enough with itself. And the characters we meet there have long ago become real characters to us, and we remember them just as we remember people in the gravest novels. The Mad Hatter, the moralizing Duchess, the angry Queen of Hearts, the doleful Mock Turtle, Tweedledum and Tweedledee, the vain and pedantic Humpty Dumpty, the Red Queen and the White Queen, and the wistful White Knight—how well we know these extraordinary people! The fun—except perhaps in one or two of the verse parodies—is never forced; indeed, strictly speaking, there is no fun at all, only a kind of grave idiocy, with everything quietly becoming madder and madder, or—as Alice herself said—curiouser and curiouser. Incidentally, Carroll's work is as a rule wrongly estimated. To begin with, we are nearly always told that *The Hunting of the Snark* is not a success. It seems to some of us a superb achievement, something unique in narrative verse. It is droll and nonsensical and yet faintly sinister, just like a dream. The Snark itself—that might or might not be a Boojum—is essentially one of those mysterious creatures that haunt the shadows of a dream. That all the members of the questing crews should all have names beginning with B, should be led by a haughty Bellman, should include a Baker who can bake nothing but Bridecake, all this, we feel, is very right and proper. This is not, by the way, a poem for children. Then it is usual to say that *Alice in Wonderland* is better than its sequel. But, for once, the sequel is the better work of art. *Through the Looking Glass* is both richer and stranger; it contains *Jabberwocky*, *The Walrus and the Carpenter*, and that poem of the White Knight's that has so many titles and is, like Wordsworth, a little crazed:

> But I was thinking of a way
> To feed oneself on batter,
> And so go on from day to day
> Getting a little fatter.
> I shook him well from side to side,
> Until his face was blue:
> "Come, tell me how you live," I cried,
> "And what is it you do?"

it has that *Wool and Water* chapter which is perhaps more like an absurd dream than anything else in literature; it has such glorious figures as Tweedledum and Tweedledee, Humpty Dumpty (who is just

like some modern poets and critics), the wistful
White Knight, and the fantastic royal personages.
It is in this tale that the genius of Lewis Carroll is at
its height; and it is a genius that compels wonder and
admiration and love from good people at all ages,
from the child who gravely follows the adventures
to the men and women who laugh to find themselves
once more tangled in its happy nonsense.

To these two names may be added a third, that of
the famous Savoyard. Gilbert's reputation is not
what it was, but it will last a long time yet. His
characteristic work does not contain much humour
proper; it is an odd mixture of satire and amusing
nonsense; and it seems laboured and acid when
compared with that of Lear or Lewis Carroll. As a
satirist he has lost force, and his admirers make a
mistake when they take their stand upon his satirical
powers. Moreover, his taste was never very certain,
and he lacks warmth and kindness. Then again, a
good deal of his fun-making is very mechanical;
much of it has a dry legal flavour; he returns time
after time to the same situations—that, for example,
of the man who acts in several different official
capacities and so discovers that he will have to arrest
himself, and so on and so forth—and his plots are,
in general, the products of a very laboured ingenuity
and do not display any particular knowledge of
human nature. *Patience* has been often praised as a
masterly satire, but indeed the two poets are only
made to look ridiculous by the situations into which
they are thrust, and two dragoons or comic librettists
would look equally ridiculous if they cut the same
capers. It is only in one or two of the songs, such as:

Then a sentimental passion of a vegetable
  fashion must excite your languid spleen,
An attachment à la Plato for a bashful young
  potato, or not-too-French French bean!
Though the Philistines may jostle, you will rank
  as an apostle in the high æsthetic band,
If you walk down Piccadilly with a poppy or a
  lily in your mediæval hand,
And every one will say,
As you walk your flowery way,
"If he's content with a vegetable love which
  would certainly not suit *me*,
Why, what a most particularly pure young man
  this pure young man must be!"

that Gilbert hits the target. Where he really excels—
setting aside the ingenuity and gusto of his rhyming
—is in his cool and almost mathematical develop-
ment of situations that are wildly absurd. All his
comic operas are a kind of trial by jury—for everybody in them elaborately argues a case—and in the
kingdom of nonsense Gilbert is Solicitor-General,
the coolest quibbler there. His satirical strokes are
contemptible when compared with his initial happy
splashes of absurdity: the sailors in *Pinafore*, at once
so strangely melodramatic and genteel; the tender-
hearted *Pirates of Penzance*; the astonishing con-
junction of fairies and the House of Lords in
Iolanthe; the vicissitudes of officials in the *Town of
Titipu*; the assembly of ghosts in *Ruddigore* that passes
resolutions in the matter of the daily crime; the dual
monarchy of *Barataria*; the unhappy conspirators
in *The Grand Duke* with their embarrassing sign:

Martha: Oh, bother the secret sign! I've eaten it until I'm quite uncomfortable! I've given it six times already to-day, and (*whimpering*) I can't eat any breakfast!

Bertha: And it's so unwholesome. Why, we should all be as yellow as frogs if it wasn't for the make-up!

Ludwig: All this is rank treason to the cause. I suffer as much as any of you. I loathe the repulsive thing—I can't contemplate it without a shudder, but I'm a conscientious conspirator, and if you won't give the sign I will. (*Eats sausage roll with an effort.*)

Lastly, whether the credit for these delightful Savoy operas must be given to the author or the composer of them, the fact remains that nothing so good in this kind has been seen on the English stage since Gilbert's time. These Victorians—and all these creators of nonsense were very Victorian—raise a smile now, but we should not forget that they made one another laugh. Or, we may borrow a concluding remark of Mr. Chesterton's on the Victorian: "Laugh at him as a limited man, a moralist, conventionalist, an opportunist, a formalist. But remember also that he was really a humorist; and may still be laughing at you."

We must now go back a few decades, passing by such minor prose humorists as Douglas Jerrold and Albert Smith, to discuss the Victorian novel. Dickens has a chapter to himself and so can be omitted here. Thackeray inevitably comes next, and he is a very difficult subject, demanding more space than we can give him. The difficulty is this, that the humour of Thackeray cannot, as it were, be disengaged. In his early work, the contributions to *Fraser's* and to *Punch*, he is a professed humorist, but it cannot be said that he is a good humorist or even a good-humoured contributor. There is about these early things of his, the *Yellowplush Papers*, *Stubb's Calendar*, *Jeames's Diary*, the *Book of Snobs*, and the rest, a certain griminess and grittiness, an underlying savagery, or at least exasperation, that makes us feel that their author is laughing on the wrong side of his face. The later contributions to *Punch*, which include the delightful parodies of the novelists already mentioned, are milder and more amusing. There are, for example, those delicious accounts of the "Ingleez" shown to the East:

> "That is the commencement of the day with thousands of English Effendis in Lundoon," the Interpreter explains. "He rises at eight. He shaves. He meets his family, kisses them, but rarely speaks, except to swear a little, and find fault. He reads through *El Tims*. He gives money to the Khanum. He goes to the Stee, where his counting-house or office of business is, and which is often a long way from his house. He goes on foot, while his wife has a chariot."

Then there are the longer burlesques, such as *A Legend of the Rhine* and *Rebecca and Rowena*; and, of course, there is *The Rose and the Ring*. In his occasional verse, too, there is some capital humour, though the best of his ballads, that of *Bouillabaisse*, is nearer tears than laughter. But, indeed, the mood

of this ballad is the prevailing mood in Thackeray's
best work, which glimmers with a humour that
cannot be easily disengaged from the satire and the
melancholy moralizing. Before the laugh is out,
the author is seen shaking his head. He has a
magnificent sense of comic character, as we see in
his Costigans and Fokers, but, unlike Dickens, he
does not indulge his droll people, does not dandle
their oddities until the characters themselves seem
twice as large as life. He smiles, winces a little,
smiles again, shrugs, then goes on unrolling his vast
hazy panorama of life and character.

Trollope has a good sense of humour, and now and
again, in the Barsetshire novels, he gives us comic
scenes that are entirely admirable. There is, for
example, that scene at the Proudie reception, in
Barchester Towers; when the poor bishop first makes
the acquaintance of Bertie Stanhope and his sister,
the Signora:

"Do you like Barchester, on the whole?" asked
Bertie.

The bishop, looking dignified, said he did like
Barchester.

"You've not been here very long, I believe,"
said Bertie.

"No—not long," said the bishop, and tried
again to make his way between the back of the
sofa and a heavy rector, who was staring over it
at the grimaces of the signora.

"You weren't a bishop before, were you?"

Dr. Proudie explained that this was the first
diocese he had held.

"Ah—I thought so," said Bertie; "but you are changed about sometimes, a'nt you?"

"Translations are occasionally made," said Dr. Proudie; "but not so frequently as in former days."

"They've cut them all down to pretty nearly the same figure, haven't they?" said Bertie.

To this the bishop could not bring himself to make any answer, but again attempted to move the rector.

"But the work, I suppose, is different?" continued Bertie. "Is there much to do here, at Barchester?" This was said exactly in the tone that a young Admiralty clerk might use in asking the same question of a brother acolyte at the Treasury.

"The work of a Bishop of the Church of England," said Dr. Proudie, with considerable dignity, "is not easy. The responsibility which he has to bear is very great indeed."

"Is it?" said Bertie, opening wide his wonderful blue eyes. "Well, I never was afraid of responsibility. I once had thoughts of being a bishop, myself."

"Had thoughts of being a bishop!" said Dr. Proudie, much amazed.

"That is, a parson—a parson first, you know, and a bishop afterwards. If I had once begun, I'd have stuck to it. But, on the whole, I like the Church of Rome the best."

The bishop could not discuss the point, so he remained silent.

"Now, there's my father," continued Bertie; "he hasn't stuck to it. I fancy he didn't like saying the same thing over so often. By the bye, Bishop, have you seen my father?"

The bishop was more amazed than ever. Had he seen his father? "No," he replied; "he had not yet had the pleasure: he hoped he might"; and, as he said so, he resolved to bear heavy on that fat, immovable rector, if ever he had the power of doing so.

"He's in the room somewhere," said Bertie, "and he'll turn up soon. By the bye, do you know much about the Jews?"

At last the bishop saw a way out. "I beg your pardon," said he; "but I'm forced to go round the room."

"Well, I believe I'll follow in your wake," said Bertie.

The whole scene is very good indeed. Trollope's danger is the facetious, and nearly all his scenes of what we might call "low life," such as those that show Johnny Eames in his London boarding-house, are ruined by heavy handling and a rather coarse facetiousness. His satirical chapters too rarely succeed in being really funny. On the whole, his weighty realism, his unfailing sobriety, his even touch, all of which make him the fine novelist he is, stand in the way of his humour. In actual life he could bellow with laughter, but in his fiction he keeps a close grip upon himself.

Mrs. Gaskell sent a ripple of humour through nearly everything she wrote, but it is, of course, in *Cranford* that she is the humorist pure and simple. *Cranford* has been described as a mixture of Dickens and Jane Austen, but, as a matter of fact, its spirit is different from either. In these sketches Mrs. Gaskell handles her subject matter more or less as Sterne did, that is, she concentrates entirely upon the humorous and the pathetic, dropping out what will neither make us laugh nor cry. This is frequently how the memory presents old scenes, and perhaps this deliberately sentimental method is only tolerable when it goes to work in the atmosphere of reminiscence. It is perhaps essential, too, that all the chief personages should be lovable and very simple, innocent, as they are in *Cranford*. How well we know these people! Captain Brown (who never ought to have been killed off so early), the wistful Miss Matty, the more belligerent Miss Pole, the tremendous Honourable Mrs. Jamieson and her sister-in-law, Lady Glenmire, who came down from the heights to marry Mr. Huggins, Miss Betsy Barker, who put her Alderney cow into grey flannel drawers, that devoted maid, Martha, who made one remark that is—or at least deserves to be—famous:

"List to reason——"
"I'll not listen to reason," she said, now in full possession of her voice, which had been rather choked with sobbing. "Reason aways means what some one else has got to say. . . ."

and that astonishing magician, Signor Brunoni, who turns out to be ex-sergeant Sam. Brown. It was just after his performance that the panic began; anything might happen after those feats of magic:

All at once all sorts of uncomfortable rumours got afloat in the town. There were one or two robberies, real *bona fide* robberies; men had up before the magistrates and committed for trial— and that seemed to make us all afraid of being robbed; and for a long time, at Miss Matty's, I know we used to make a regular expedition all round the kitchens and cellars every night, Miss Matty leading the way, armed with the poker, I following with the hearth-brush, and Martha carrying the shovel and fireirons with which to sound the alarm; and by the accidental hitting together of them she often frightened us so much that we bolted ourselves up, all three together, in the back-kitchen, or store-room, or wherever we happened to be, till, when our affright was over, we recollected ourselves, and set out afresh with double valiance. By day we heard strange stories from the shopkeepers and cottagers, of carts that went about in the dead of night, drawn by horses shod with felt, and guarded by men in dark clothes, going round the town, no doubt in search of some unwatched house or some unfastened door.

Miss Pole, who affected great bravery herself, was the principal person to collect and arrange these reports so as to make them assume their most fearful aspect. But we discovered that she had begged one of Mr. Huggins' worn-out hats to hang up in her lobby, and we (at least I) had doubts as to whether she really would enjoy the little adventure of having her house broken into, as she protested she should. Miss Matty made no secret of being an arrant coward, but she went regularly through her housekeeper's duty of inspection, only the hour for this became earlier and earlier,

till at last we went the rounds at half-past six, and
Miss Matty adjourned to bed soon after seven, "in
order to get the night over the sooner."

This *Cranford* seems to have been the parent of many
quaint and remote villages, seen through a haze of
reminiscence, and there must be included among
them one called Thrums, which stands outside this
chronicle. A whole host have appeared in America,
where such villages appear to look out on a river
of molasses and maple syrup. Indeed, Mrs. Gaskell
initiated a whole school of literature with this little
classic of sentimental humour, though it is doubtful
if she would have regarded its works with any
favour could she have lived to see them.

There are two novelists of the later nineteenth
century whose humour seems to some of us to have
been greatly over-praised. The first is George Eliot.
That her close studies of provincial and rural folk
do contain a good deal of genuine humour, we do
not deny. Curiously enough, for we should never
have expected it of this very clever self-conscious
woman, with her rather solemn culture, she is at her
best as a humorist in dealing with very muddle-
headed persons, like the rustic wits and philosophers
who forgather at the Rainbow Inn:

> "Ay, but there's this in it, Dowlais," said the
> landlord, speaking in a tone of much candour and
> tolerance. "There's folks, i' my opinion, they can't
> see ghos'es, not if they stood as plain as a pikestaff
> before 'em. And there's reason i' that. For there's
> my wife, now, can't smell, not if she'd the strongest
> o' cheese under her nose. I never see'd a ghost

myself; but then I says to myself—Very like I haven't got the smell for 'em. I mean, putting a ghost for a smell, or else contrariways. And so, I'm for holding for both sides; for, as I say, the truth lies between 'em. An' if Dowlais was to go and stand and say he'd never seen a wink of Cliff's Holiday all the night through, I'd back him; and if anybody said as Cliff's Holiday was certain sure for all that, I'd back *him* too. For the smell's what I go by."

She handles such people amazingly well. But too much of her humour is nothing but a laboured facetiousness. Her feelings do not run easily enough, there is too great a sense of strain in her for her to be a humorist of any importance. And in her later work there is hardly a flicker of fun. The other novelist is George Meredith. Now Meredith has wit in abundance, crackles and sparkles with it continuously, but he has very little real humour. A strong dose of mingled humility and affection (both of which he plainly lacks) might have turned him into a great humorist, for he has all the necessary high spirits, gusto, and lightning powers of observation. He did acutally come near to creating two great comic figures in the Countess de Saldar and Richmond Roy, and there are capital outbursts of high spirits in most of the novels. But his atmosphere is too rare and arid for the successful cultivation of genuine humour: he gives us the cactus of philosophical wit, and, seeing that we have little of it in our literature, we must be thankful.

The world that Hardy presents in his fiction is a

much more gloomy affair than anything George Eliot or Meredith shows us, but nevertheless it is enriched at times by a humour that neither of them ever achieves. It is a rustic, almost earthy humour, made up chiefly of the slow talk of quaint, remote characters, whose every speech is rich and strange and yet always completely convincing. We have only to dip into such a tale as his *Under the Greenwood Tree* to discover these personages:

"Times have changed from the times they used to be," said Mail, regarding nobody can tell what interesting old panoramas with an inward eye, and letting his outward glance rest on the ground, because it was as convenient a position as any. "People don't care much about us now! I've been thinking, we must be almost the last left in the county of the old string-players. Barrel-organs, and they next door to 'em that you blow wi' your foot, have come in terribly of late years."

"Ah!" said Bowman, shaking his head; and old William, on seeing him, did the same thing.

"More's the pity," replied another. "Time was —long and merry ago now—when not one of the varmits was to be heard of; but it served some of the choirs right. They should have stuck to strings as we did, and keep out clar'nets, and done away with serpents. If you'd thrive in musical religion, stick to strings, says I."

"Strings are well enough, as far as that goes," said Mr. Spinks.

"There's worse things than serpents," said Mr. Penny. "Old things pass away, 'tis true; but a

H

serpent was a good old note; a deep rich note was the serpent."

"Clar'nets, however, be bad at all times," said MichaelMail. "One Christmas—yearsagone now, years—I went the rounds wi' the Dibbeach choir. 'Twas a hard frosty night, and the keys of all the clar'nets froze—ah, they did freeze—so that 'twas like drawing a cork every time a key was opened; the players o' 'em had to go into a hedger and ditcher's chimley-corner, and thaw their clar'nets every now and then. An icicle o' spet hung down from the end of every man's clar'net a span long; and as to fingers—well, there, if ye'll believe men, we had no fingers at all, to our knowledge."

"I can well bring back to my mind," said Mr. Penny, "what I said to poor Joseph Ryme (who took the tribble part in High-Story Church for two-and-forty year) when they thought of having clar'nets there. 'Joseph,' I said, says I, 'depend upon't, if so be you have them tooting clar'nets you'll spoil the whole set-out. Clar'nets were not made for the service of Providence; you can see it by looking at 'em,' I said. And what cam o't? Why, my dear souls, the parson set up a barrel-organ on his own account within two years o' the time I spoke, and the old choir went to nothing."

"As far as look is concerned," said the tranter, "I don't for my part see that a fiddle is much nearer heaven than a clar'net. 'Tis farther off. There's always a rakish, scampish countenance about a fiddle that seems to say the Wicked One had a hand in making o'en; while angels be supposed to play clar'nets in heaven, or som'at like 'em, if ye may believe picters."

There is genius in some of these phrases. What could be better than "long and merry ago now!" These are the best humorous rustics we have had since Shakespeare. Few novelists of these days are lucky enough to be within sight of such characters, within hearing of such talk, all so racy of the soil, so charged with humour. It is rather surprising that Hardy had to quarrel so bitterly with a universe that offered him, among other things, such people and such enchanting talk.

At the time when Hardy was bringing out his later novels there was much talk of "the New Humour." There had been, it seems, a revolution in jesting, but what this revolution effected, what was thrown down and what was set up, is now something of a mystery. *Punch* went on his way, now under the guidance of F. C. Burnand, a desperate punster, whose best work is to be found in *Happy Thoughts*. The most popular contributor was probably "F. Anstey," who made a very large public happy with his fantastic farcical tales, such as *Vice Versa* and *The Brass Bottle*, but whose humour is most deftly displayed in such collections of dialogues as *Voces Populi*. It was in *Punch*, too, that there first appeared that little masterpiece of humour, *The Diary of a Nobody*, by the brothers Grossmith. Are there people who are still unacquainted with Mr. Pooter and his family, with Cummings and Gowing, with Burwin-Fosselton of the Holloway Comedians, and Mr. Padge, who never says anything but "That's right," and yet contrives to be a tremendous character? If so, we can only pity them. This little book is in the old tradition of English humour: it is full of the most gorgeous fooling, but it is something more than merely funny; there is in it a sort of tenderness; poor Mr. Pooter, with his little vanities, his simplicity, his timidity, his goodness of heart, is not simply a figure of fun, but one of those innocent, lovable fools who are dear to the heart. Lamb would have loved Mr. Pooter and his naïve confessions. Jerome K. Jerome never did anything as good as *The Diary of a Nobody*. His *Three Men in a Boat*, which was, of course, immensely popular, was on a very much lower level of humour altogether and is full of that mechanical fun-making which Mark Twain and other Americans had introduced into this country some time before. But if Jerome was over-praised by one section of the public, he was also rather unfairly treated by another section, and certainly never deserved the "'Arry K. 'Arry" that *Punch* gave him. He had a real sense of humour, and it may be discovered at its best, though mixed with a good deal of rather maudlin sentiment, in his semi-autobiographical novel, *Paul Kelver*. He was, too, an extraordinarily good editor, and gathered round him a number of young men who soon showed great promise as humorists. Among these were Mr. Pett Ridge and Mr. Barry Pain, and, best of all, Mr. W. W. Jacobs. Mr. Jacobs is both a genuine artist and a genuine humorist. His little tales are models of deft manipulation, in which there is never a word too much; and in these things he gives us excellent comic plots, very carefully worked out, and any amount of droll by-play. He never raises his voice, and is perhaps the slyest of all our humorists. This is his manner:

> "I got to know about it through knowing the servant that lived there. A nice, quiet gal she was, and there wasn't much went on that she didn't hear. I've known 'er to cry for hours with the earache, pore gal. . . ."

or this:

> "—What are you going to say, Harry?"
> "The truth," said the solicitor virtuously.
> "So am I," said his friend; "but mind, we must both tell the same tale, whatever it is. . . ."

His command of his material is so perfect that he makes it all look easy, but the fact remains that nobody else has ever been able to do quite what he does. And that he is a genuine artist is further proved by the fact that he has contrived to create a tiny world of his own; there is a definite W. W. Jacobs world, and most of us cannot be grateful enough for all the little happy holidays we have spent in it.

We are now among living men, and must stop our galloping and gossiping. We have no great English humorist to show at the present time, but, nevertheless, humour is still with us. There is the delicate fantastic humour of Max, at its best in *Zuleika Dobson* and *Seven Men*. There is Mr. G. K. Chesterton, with his uproarious intellectual high spirits, a figure as English as a plum pudding and as welcome. Among the older novelists, there is Mr. H. G. Wells, who can sometimes write as if he had not the ghost of a sense of humour, but who at other times, in *Kipps* and *Mr. Polly*, for example, has given us chapters of the most delightful humorous writing, Dickensian in their exuberance. There are such *Punch* men as Messrs A. A. Milne, E. V. Knox, A. P. Herbert, who happily range from stage comedies to light verse, essays to parodies; and among the humorous journalists there is the very original and gravely fantastic Mr. D. B. Wyndham Lewis. There is Mr. P. G. Wodehouse, who can conjure out of sheer inanity and speechlessness a pleasant light humour that is all his own. No doubt there are many others, and no doubt we have omitted to mention all manner of important persons; but it cannot be helped. We have come a long way in a little time, having rushed from Chaucer's *Tabard* down the laughing centuries to the *Potwell Inn*, where Mr. Polly is sitting in the tap, and now are fairly blown and must call a halt.

CHAPTER VI

THREE NOVELISTS

THAT Fielding is one of our great novelists, one of the very greatest, is a fact only denied by those who have never read him or by those who have not the sense to understand him. Anybody, in truth, ought to be able to enjoy his bustle of event, variety of character, and high spirits, but it happens that many people who read (and sometimes pronounce judgment in print upon what they read) know very little about life and are not disposed to admire Fielding simply because they are in no position to appreciate his massive knowledge of human nature. He is essentially a masculine writer; a man with a large cool mind. His works are so robust and enduring, not because—as Thackeray would seem to believe—he himself was a hearty fellow, but because they have any amount of intellectual bone and sinew in them. The author upon whom he modelled himself as a novelist was Cervantes, and, therefore, it is not surprising that his characteristic vein should be one of grave irony. He had a taste, which his age shared, for scenes of the roughest horseplay, pothouse scuffles, and female scratching matches and the like, and it was his pleasure to describe these scenes at length in a mock-epic style. This is his humour at its lowest level, and there must be few readers who do not find it tiresome. A long account of an alehouse row is not made any the less tedious by such comments as:"Now the dogs of war being let loose, began to lick their bloody lips; now Victory, with golden wings, hung hovering in the air. . . ." At the other extreme from this pedantic buffoonery is the very grim irony of *Jonathan Wild*, an astonishing intellectual feat, but not one to everybody's taste. High above both is the delightful ironic humour that may be found everywhere in *Tom Jones* and *Amelia*, but that is at its best in *Joseph Andrews*, playing like summer lightning round the figure of Parson Adams.

The good parson is a comic-heroic figure, an English cousin of Don Quixote. Fielding loves him —and makes us love him—because of his courage and innocence and essential goodness of heart, and he bestrides the plot like a Colossus, but that does not mean that he is at all exempted from the novelist's ironic humour. At first we are asked to laugh, gently, at his innocence and absence of mind. How delightful is the affair of the sermons! He is taking them to London in a bag! He is taking them to London in a bag, and tries to borrow money with them as security. "There were in that bag no less than nine volumes of manuscript sermons, as well worth a hundred pounds as a shilling was worth twelve-pence." But the landlord will not accept such security, and then Adams learns from a fellow parson and a bookseller that sermons are a drug on the market. This does not deter him. What does is the discovery that there are no sermons in the bag at all, his wife having replaced them by shirts and other useful articles. Much better, however, is that talk with Wilson, who tells his story and enlarges on the subject of "that worst of passions"—vanity:

"My second remark was (Wilson is speaking), that vanity is the worst of passions, and more apt to contaminate the mind than any other: for as selfishness is much more general than we please to allow it, so it is natural to hate and envy those who stand between us and the good we desire. Now, in lust and ambition, these are few; and even in avarice we find many who are no obstacles to our pursuits; but the vain man seeks pre-eminence; and everything which is excellent or praiseworthy in another renders him the mark of his antipathy. Adams now began to fumble in his pockets, and soon cried out, 'Oh la! I have it not about me.' Upon this the gentleman asking him what he was searching for, he said he searched after a sermon, which he thought his masterpiece, against vanity. 'Fie upon it, fie upon it!' cries he, 'why do I ever leave that sermon out of my pocket? I wish it was within five miles; I would willingly fetch it to read it you.' The gentleman answered there was no need, for he was cured of the passion. 'And for that very reason,' quoth Adams, 'I would read it, for I am confident you would admire it; indeed, I have never been a greater enemy to any passion than that silly one of vanity.'"

The full force of this famous little scene has hardly ever been appreciated. It is amusing that Adams should be vain enough to be ready to walk ten miles in order that his companion might admire his sermon

denouncing vanity, but it is better still that Wilson
should merely smile, as we are told he did, at this
display of what he calls "the worst of passions." It
is obvious that vanity is not the worst of passions;
and they are a pair of noodles. There are, too, some
very fine strokes of ironic humour in that scene
which takes place at an alehouse, where Adams
meets a priest in layman's dress. The two of them
take turns in denouncing the love of money and in
declaring their contempt for riches. Then the priest
asks Adams for the loan of eighteenpence to pay his
bill, but Adams discovers that his pocket has been
picked and he is penniless. The other clearly does
not believe him, but manages to persuade the landlord to let the bill stand as a debit, and quickly
departs:

> He was no sooner gone than the host fell
> a-shaking his head, and declared, if he had sus-
> pected the fellow had no money, he would not
> have drawn him a single drop of drink, saying he
> despaired of ever seeing his face again, for that he
> looked like a confounded rogue. "Rabbit the
> fellow," cries he, "I thought, by his talking so
> much riches, that he had a hundred pounds at
> least in his pocket." Adams chid him for his
> suspicions, which, he said, were not becoming a
> Christian; and then, without reflecting on his loss,
> or considering how he himself should depart in
> the morning, he retired to a very homely bed, as
> his companions had before.

Then there is that delightful long scene towards
the end of the book in which Adams rebukes Joseph

for his impatience to be married. He produces quite a sermon on such topics as marriage, fear as a want of confidence in the Supreme Being, the danger of setting the affections absolutely on a fellow creature; but, unfortunately, in the middle of it, a person rushes in to tell him that his youngest son is drowned. Immediately Adams is overcome with sorrow, and Joseph in his turn tries to comfort him and even uses some of his own arguments. Adams will have none of it:

"Child, child," said he, "do not go about impossibilities. Had it been any other of my children, I could have borne it with patience; but my little prattler, the darling and comfort of my old age, the little wretch, to be snatched out of life just at his entrance into it; the sweetest, best-tempered boy, who never did a thing to offend..."

However, the boy is not drowned, and the joy of Adams is now as wild as his grief had been. But when he has calmed down, he turns moralist again, and tells Joseph that he must not give way too easily to his earthly affections. Joseph points out that it is easier to give this kind of advice than to act upon it. Adams retorts by declaring that Joseph does not understand the tenderness of fatherly affection and that the loss of a child is an unusually great trial. Joseph counters by saying that it may be as bad to lose a well-beloved mistress, so that Adams, cornered, has to strike out with:

"Yes, but such love is foolishness and wrong in itself, and ought to be conquered; it savours too much of the flesh." "Sure, sir," says Joseph, "it is not sinful to love my wife, no, not even to doat upon her to distraction!" "Indeed, but it is," says Adams: "Every man ought to love his wife, no doubt; we are commanded to do so; but we ought to love her with moderation and discretion." "I am afraid I shall be guilty of some sin in spite of all my endeavours," says Joseph; "for I shall love without any moderation, I am sure." "You talk foolishly and childishly," cried Adams. "Indeed," says Mrs. Adams, who had listened to the latter part of their conversation, "you talk more foolishly yourself. I hope, my dear, you will never preach any such doctrines as that husbands can love their wives too well. If I knew you had such a sermon in the house, I am sure I would burn it; and I declare, if I had not been convinced you had loved me as well as you could, I can answer for myself, I should have hated and dispised you. Marry, come up! Fine doctrine indeed! . . ."

We can leave Adams in such good hands. Throughout all this we see Fielding's habit of contrasting preaching and practice, our codes and our actual impulses; but with Parson Adams it happens for once that what is felt and done is better than what is merely thought, and though the irony is there it is no longer grim but sunny and humorous. The full stature of Parson Adams is not, of course, to be measured by such extracts as these. There, in the full story, with his old wig and torn cassock, his cool ethics and warm heart, he lives, not merely moves and talks, lives as only the great personages of fiction do, and we laugh at him as we would at some queer, lovable, old friend.

There may be more laughable works in English literature than *Tristram Shandy*, but there is none more strictly humorous. It is one gigantic whim or, rather, nest of whims, enclosing one another like those Oriental balls or boxes. It is a humorous vision of this life. The narrative neither starts from anywhere nor arrives anywhere; it does not travel at all but merely contorts itself. The whole affair seems to be outside time. Sterne's masterpiece is a complete entity—true to its one law that there shall not be any laws observed—but nevertheless we may recognize that it contains humour on a good many different levels. At the lowest level are all the silly tricks that need the help of the printer—the blank or blackened pages, and the dots and dashes. At the highest level is the humour that plays about the figures of the Shandy family and their associates. These people are droll in themselves, and their relations with one another make them droller still. The most famous of them is, of course, Uncle Toby, but actually Tristram's father, Walter Shandy, is just as good. Nor are Mrs. Shandy and Corporal Trim far behind. Mr. Shandy is an amateur philosopher, who prides himself on his power of reasoning and dislikes a simple explanation of anything. He is sowing his intellectual wild oats late in life, which is all the worse for him. He is full of out-of-the-way learning, fine-spun theories, grand paradoxes, magnificent chains of reasoning, intellectual curiosity and love of debate, and only wants common sense. Unfortunately he has no audience. His wife and his brother do not understand what he is talking about and do not very much care, having no intellectual curiosity, not the least glimmering of ideas, themselves. As Coleridge points out, the essence of Mr. Shandy's character:

> Is a craving for sympathy in exact proportion to the oddity and unsympathizability of what he proposes; this coupled with an instinctive desire to be at least disputed with, or rather both in one, to dispute and yet to agree, and, holding, as worst of all, to acquiesce, without either resistance or sympathy. . . .

Now, Mrs. Shandy, if the matter is some practical concern, always has her mind made up and cannot be persuaded to change it, but if the matter does not come home to her, she simply agrees with, without ever understanding, what her husband says. Thus poor Mr. Shandy is as irritated as an enthusiastic pianist might be who found himself for ever among deaf people. Sterne makes great play with this misfortune of his:

> It was a consuming vexation to my father, that my mother never asked the meaning of a thing she did not understand.
> That she is not a woman of science, my father would say—is her misfortune—but she might ask a question.
> My mother never did. In short, she went out of the world at last without knowing whether it turned round or stood still. My father had

officiously told her above a thousand times which way it was, but she always forgot. . . .

And Uncle Toby is as annoying a companion for this baffled expositor as his wife. He is perhaps worse, because at times it does appear for a moment that he is about to be interested, and Mr. Shandy's hopes rise only to be quickly dashed again. This is what happened when Mr. Shandy, seeing a chance for a dissertation, began by remarking that the two hours he and Toby had waited seemed an age:

'Tis owing entirely, quoth my Uncle Toby, to the succession of our ideas.

My father, who had an itch, in common with all philosophers, of reasoning upon everything which happened, and accounting for it, too—proposed infinite pleasure to himself in this, of the succession of ideas, and had not the least apprehension of having it snatched out of his hands by my Uncle Toby, who (honest man!) generally took every thing as it happened; and who, of all things in the world, troubled his brain least with abstruse thinking . . . my father knew it—and was no less surprised than he was disappointed, with my uncle's fortuitous solution.

"Do you understand the theory of that affair?" replied my father.

"No, I," quoth my uncle.

"But you have some ideas," said my father, "of what you talk about?"

"No more than my horse," replied my Uncle Toby.

Mr. Shandy can do nothing in face of such cheerful ignorance. Toby remains impervious and indifferent until he hears his brother mention a succession of ideas that follow one another like a train, and then he cuts in at once with "A train of artillery." For Toby takes everything literally, and relates all he hears to his own experience, almost entirely military. When his brother, in despair when he learns that his son's nose has been crushed, asks if ever a poor, unfortunate man received so many lashes, Toby replies at once that the most he ever saw given were to a grenadier in Mackay's regiment, and rings the bell for his corporal, Trim, to verify the reference. Toby is all simplicity and affection, and he and his corporal and their mimic sieges on the bowling green are unforgettable. He is as solid as a hill.

Toby is just as much absorbed in his reminiscences of the war and his miniature sieges as his brother is in his theories and fine chains of reasoning. In truth, these Shandies cannot understand one another at all, and half the fun comes from their baffled attempts to communicate one with another. There is more here than the time-old trick of making a number of comic characters out of so many ruling passions, the every-man-in-his-humour business. Sterne might have made a very grim satire on this life if he had confined himself to showing how these persons (who are not so very different from the rest of us) were each shut up in the little painted box of their minds and could do no more than wave despairingly out of the window. The satire would be strengthened, too, by his emphasis—which may be seen almost throughout the book—on the fact that we are horribly dependent upon little things being right and, proud creatures that we are, find ourselves at the mercy of door-hinges and window-sashes. Not a little of the drollery of the book turns on the way in which everything is being continually held up because of some tiny accident. The reason that we do not feel that the book is a despairing satire upon this life is because it is never for long a purely intellectual affair. It is steeped in sentiment. The Shandies may not understand one another, but, nevertheless, they love one another. They may not share one another's thoughts but they always share one another's feelings. They are all loving and lovable. For this reason alone, they are not figures of satire—and no man in his sense ever imagined they were—but figures of pure humour.

It we take the sentiment (though, of course, we cannot take it out because it is part of the man), Sterne seems extraordinarily modern. Coleridge noted that the first of his excellencies consists:

> In bringing forward into distinct conscious-
> ness those minutiæ of thought and feeling which
> appear trifles, yet have an importance for the
> moment, and which almost every man feels in one
> way or other. . . .

This is precisely what the most recent school of novelists is engaged in doing. A great deal of the most characteristic modern fiction is simply made up of the "minutiæ of thought and feeling." Many of our novelists join with Sterne in showing us how the mind, so proud and apparently free, is hampered

I

by its clumsy, fumbling companion, the body, how we are for ever baffled by the most absurd little accidents, how every little flicker of thought or feeling turns us this way and that. Yet it is only by making an effort that we can realize that this likeness exists at all, for *Tristram Shandy* and one of the clever but depressingly bleak fictions of to-day seem whole worlds away from one another. Our contemporaries achieve a sort of crackle of thin, bitter laughter, but not humour. The difference between them and Sterne is this, that they leave out affection and do not succeed in creating character. They give us the Shandy accidents and bewilderment, but not the Shandy affection and the sharp edges of character that make "My Father" and "My Uncle Toby" so memorable. In order to be a humorist, you must have a needle eye for the incongruities, the pretensions, the inconsistencies, all the idiocies and antics of this life, but you must also have—strange and contradictory as it may seem—an unusual quickness and warmth of feeling, an instant affection for all that is lovable. We have many writers now who have the needle eye, and many, too, who have the depth of affection, but until we find them both in the same man we shall look in vain for a great humorist.

To go from Sterne to Jane Austen is to make a long journey, for it is to go from a very excitable man, laughing and crying in one breath, to a very cool woman, delicately and deliciously raising her eyebrows. It is not our business here to discuss the quiet perfection of art that Jane Austen brought into fiction. That lies outside our province. But she has

humour, an abundance of it, and that humour
happens to be easily the best specimen of its kind we
have. Its kind is that belonging to the cool feminine
temper, which expresses itself by way of irony, and
is the terror of all comfortable egoistical males. She
deliberately restricted herself to a very limited
sphere, content to observe what went on round the
tea-table, during a walk across the park, at the local
ball, but within that sphere she missed nothing.

Her humour circles about characters, and it cannot
be said that they are always characters she likes, or
rather people she likes, for strictly as characters she
enjoys them. Perhaps this is the secret. Her delight
in their absurdity runs away with her a little, and so
she indulges them and becomes humorous instead
of being satirical. This is certainly true of Mr.
Collins, the comic character she has limned with
most gusto, who in his magnificence of folly is really
a creature of greater stature than any of her other
figures, one who looks forward and backward to the
gods and giants of drollery that are the creation of
Dickens and Shakespeare. Like most of the great
Dickens characters, Mr. Collins is not very funny
in the *idea* of him, in the bare bones of his character,
for literature is full of such snobs and toadies; it is in
the actual expression of himself that he becomes so
funny. At the same time, snobbery and toadyism in
him are raised to such a height that they almost
acquire the innocence of some great youthful
passion. Mr. Collins may admire mean things—for
his own paltry preferment and his Lady Catherine de
Bourgh are hardly ideal objects—but we cannot say
that he admires them meanly. When he remembers

(and he never really forgets for more than two minutes) his position at Hunsford, Ladyne's Catheri invitations to dinner, and her quadrille table, her condescending interest in the cupboards of the parsonage, he is lost in a kind of happy wonder. This is to be no ordinary snob: it is simply to be the victim of a successful grand passion. Small wonder that he should not be in love with the ladies he proposes to, he is already in love with his own astonishing position and Lady Catherine's affability and the delights of Rosings: there is no room left for any further passion and ecstasy. The fact that he is both a young man and a clergyman, too, makes this extraordinary passion more ludicrous than it would otherwise be; nevertheless the fun really begins when he comes to express himself, in his actual and inimitable turn of phrase. Who could resist his reply to Mr. Bennet when the two of them are discussing the little flattering things he is in the habit of saying to Lady Catherine:

"These are the little things that please her ladyship, and it is a sort of attention which I feel myself peculiarly bound to pay.

"You judge very properly," said Mr. Bennet, 'and it is happy for you that you possess the talent of flattering with delicacy. May I ask whether these pleasing attentions proceed from the impulse of the moment, or are the result of previous study?"

"They arise chiefly from what is passing at the time, and though I sometimes amuse myself with suggesting and arranging such little elegant compliments as may be adapted to ordinary occasions, I always wish to give them as unstudied an air as possible."

It is a mystery why Mr. Bennet, that connoisseur of the absurd, ever tired of such a glorious simpleton. For, after all, what is chiefly remarkable in Mr. Collins is his simplicity, his happy innocence. When he tells Mrs. Bennet that Elizabeth has refused him, and she replies that Lizzy is a very headstrong, foolish girl, what could be more innocent than his immediate remark that "if she is really headstrong and foolish, I know not whether she would be a very desirable wife to a man in my situation, who naturally looks for happiness in the marriage state?" His actual proposal to Elizabeth is easily the best comic proposal in literature. There are discovered at their best his pompous absurdity, his innocent self-approval, his bland lack of understanding of all other persons, his idiotic rationality based on a topsy-turvy scale of values. Did ever a person set to work so methodically to bungle an affair as Mr. Collins does when he says that before his feelings run away with him on the subject, he will state his reasons for marrying, and proceeds to do so:

"My reasons for marrying are, first, that I think it a right thing for every clergyman in easy circumstances (like myself) to set the example of matrimony in his parish; secondly, that I am convinced it will add very greatly to my happiness; and, thirdly, which perhaps I ought to have mentioned earlier, that it is the particular advice and recommendation of the very noble lady whom I have the honour of calling patroness. . . ."

And thereafter, with every sentence, alienates his listener and commends himself to the rest of us for ever. Perhaps Mr. Collins, secure in the strong citadel of his folly, is the happiest and most poetical character in all Jane Austen. He comes to visit the Bennets as if he were being entertained by Sardanapalus, ready to admire and wonder at everything. Back at his own place of Hunsford, he walks about as if he were in fairyland: the very sight of Rosings through the trees leaves him happy, and a phaeton stopping at the gate, an invitation to dinner ("an invitation, moreover, including the whole party"), fill him with ecstasy. He may bore other people, but nothing bores him. Happy Mr. Collins!

Jane Austen created other comic figures, but she never indulged any of them as she did Mr. Collins. Poor Miss Bates, in *Emma*, has some kinship with Mr. Collins. She does not know what it is to be bored, though her companions do. The mere whispers of life that fall to her lot leave her breathless with excitement. A party is an almost suffocating experience, and she can only relieve her feelings by a torrent of ejaculations:

"So very obliging of you! No rain at all. Nothing to signify. I do not care for myself. Quite thick shoes. And Jane declares—Well! (as soon as she was within the door), "well! This is brilliant indeed! This is admirable! Excellently contrived, upon my word. Nothing wanting.

Could not have imagined it. So well lighted up!
Jane, Jane, look! did you ever see anything——?
Oh! Mr. Weston, you must really have had
Aladdin's lamp. Good Mrs. Stokes would not
know her own room again. I saw her as I came
in; she was standing in the entrance. 'Oh! Mrs.
Stokes,' said I—but I had not time for more. . . ."

We have all met Miss Bates. At the other extreme
from such characters, who contrive to be excited
about nothing, are people like Mr. Woodhouse
(*Emma*) and Lady Bertram (*Mansfield Park*), who
refuse to be excited about anything. Lady Bertram
seems as near nullity as it is possible for a human
being to be; her whole life is spent sitting on a sofa,
doing a little fancywork or fondling a poodle; she
has no ideas, no opinions, no tastes, no conversation,
hardly a movement; yet she is a character; we feel
that she really exists and we like to read about her.
It is Jane Austen's peculiar triumph that she can
create characters out of such materials, characters
that we can enjoy in her pages though we should
run screaming from them in real life. Mr. Woodhouse is as quiet as Lady Bertram, and it is a pity
they are in different books: they would have made
an admirable pair of friends, that is, if one of them
could have been induced to go and see the other.
Mr. Woodhouse is easily the most amusing of all
valetudinarians. If ever a man took to heart the
doctor's advice to "live quietly," it was Mr. Woodhouse. His horror of parties and late hours, of a
good dinner, of change or events of any kind; his
belief in Mr. Perry, the local doctor; his constant

apprehension, turning a slight shower of rain into a typhoon—how well we come to know these absurd little characteristics! Highbury would not be itself without him. What an agony of mind was his when his daughter's governess and friend, Miss Taylor, was married from his own house. There was all that horrible wedding-cake to be eaten. Mr. Perry himself, on being pressed, admitted that it might disagree with many people unless taken moderately. Mr. Woodhouse had not a peaceful moment until the cake was done:

There was a strange rumour in Highbury of all the little Perrys being seen with a slice of Mrs. Weston's wedding-cake in their hands; but Mr. Woodhouse would never believe it.

There is a very fine sketch of a comic character in what is perhaps Jane Austen's most exquisite story, *Persuasion*. If she had indulged Sir Walter Elliot as she indulged Mr. Collins, there would have been nothing to choose between them, but in the later story her art would not allow her to let folly go its own way unchecked. The result is that Sir Walter is only given a few moments in which to express his foolish self. But his few snatches of talk have a fine savour, the very accents of bland self-approval. We are introduced to him when he is admiring his family entry in the *Peerage*, and after that we know what to expect. Stunted as he is, however, like most genuine comic figures he contrives to better our expectations. Consider his brief condemnation of the naval profession:

"The profession has its utility, but I should be sorry to see any friend of mine belonging to it."

"Indeed!" was the reply, and with a look of surprise.

"Yes; it is in two points offensive to me; I have two strong grounds of objection to it. First, as being the means of bringing persons of obscure birth into undue distinction, and raising men to honours which their fathers and grandfathers never dreamt of; and, secondly, as it cuts up a man's youth and vigour most horribly; a sailor grows old sooner than any other man; I have observed it all my life. A man is in greater danger in the navy of being insulted by the rise of one whose father his father might have disdained to speak to, and of becoming prematurely an object of disgust himself, than in any other line. . . ."

This is very good indeed, like all Jane Austen's humour, which is never quite like anybody else's. On the other hand, it is not really the best of her. Her real triumph is the happy perfection of her art, upon which humour plays like the sunlight upon some flawless antique marble.

CHAPTER VII

CHARLES LAMB

EVEN if he had never written a single essay,
Lamb would still have deserved a chapter to
himself in this volume. His essays are no more than
little peepholes into his life, letting us see the fountain
of humour for ever playing there. They do not
merely give him readers, but perpetually enlarge the
circle of his friends. That is why we come to spend
more time at last with the letters than with the
essays; it is not a question of literary merit; the
letters bring us a step or two closer to the man, and
that is sufficient for us. Nor can we ever read
enough about him. As Raleigh once remarked—
"Charles Lamb was not a poet, or essayist, or critic—
he was a person." We cannot bring the solemn
hocus-pocus, the better-than-this and not-so-good-
as-that, of the literary historian or critic to bear upon
any account of his reputation; he is not an author
charging posterity with a regiment of works; he is
simply Charles Lamb for ever making more and
more friends. He walks down the years, this little
stammering man in black, accompanied by a
roundelay of affectionate praise. All those who knew
him—and Thomas Carlyle did not know him—felt
the better for knowing him, and those of us, a great
host, who feel that we, too, know him, in spite of the
gulfs and mists of time, find ourselves ensnared by

the same sweet influences, and pass on his name to others as that of a dear friend. English humour at his deepest and tenderest seems in him incarnate; he did not merely create it, he lived it.

His humour was not an idle thing, but the white flower plucked from a most dangerous nettle. His adult life begins in tragedy, in Elizabethan crimson and black, murder and madness and despair. He comes swaying, a grave and sensitive youth, out of a great darkness. Henceforward his whole life must be deliberately controlled, dedicated to certain ends. He must walk down a narrow channel, where there is for him neither marriage nor children, neither personal freedom nor the promise of gratified ambition, a long straight way with a grave at the end of it. His days must be spent at the office desk, and his nights with that sister to whom his life was dedicated, that sister who was for ever wandering back again into the dark of madness. When the two of them knew the shadows were closing round her again, he would take her to the asylum: they would be seen going there together arm-in-arm, weeping. To live such a life is to walk the world without a skin. Compared with this, the troubles of a roaring Thomas Carlyle, who could contemptuously dismiss the rickety tomfool, were mere thistledown. And Lamb lived this life without a murmur, thinking himself the least ill-used of his circle, and always with sympathy and good counsel and guineas to spare for his acquaintance. They themselves knew his worth. Even the formal and rather priggish Wordsworth, who had seen Lamb tipsy more than once, who was there when Lamb insisted upon feeling the bumps of that other Commissioner of Stamps, who had even had his nose pulled by Lamb and been called: "You old Lake poet! You rascally poet!" can call him "the frolic and the gentle," and declare:

O, he was good, if e'er a good man lived!

We have to remember this long, straight, narrow way he walked when we consider his humour. He began with an apparent sad sanity that masked gulfs of madness. He ended with an apparent gay insanity, a devotion to pure whimsy, that masks an exquisite sanity, a balance of so many different and dangerous forces. There were always within him depths of suffering that he never consciously revealed, though behind many a phrase of his we catch a glimpse of the darkness. Did he not say: "My waking life has much of the confusion, the trouble, and obscure perplexity of an ill dream. In the daytime I stumble upon dark mountains." He clung to what was near and homely and bright with affection. He could not sit and think; he once said: "Books think for me"; though actually few men have thought more wisely about books. He was in a position to bring things to a sharp test, and that is one reason why he is such a fine critic. He can talk of books like one who has read them by the light of a solitary candle in a great darkness. There is in him not a grain of the formal nonsense of the library, the platform, and the schools. He walked out of his tragedy freed for ever from all conventionality, hollow pretence, egoism. He was compelled to live by the steady light of his affections, and there never was a heart so securely anchored, but his wits, so sharp and bright, and his Ariel-like fancy, could wander where they pleased, had licence to juggle with earth and stars, and it is from this combination that his unique humour springs.

There is nothing more characteristic of Lamb than that story which tells how when he was asked if he knew a certain person whose character and reputation he had been attacking, he replied: "Know him! Of course I don't know him. I never could hate anyone I knew." He was quite prepared cheerfully to damn the unknown, as when the lady bored him by praising at great length "a charming man," and ended at last by exclaiming: "I know him, bless him!"; and Lamb replied: "Well, I don't, but damn him, at a hazard." Of the poet L. E. L., he declared: "If she belonged to me I would lock her up and feed her on bread and water till she left off writing poetry." His dislike of the unknown is whimsical, humorous; his love of the known and familiar is deep and abiding. This is seen in his feeling for places. No man ever cared less about travel. He writes to Wordsworth:

Separate from the pleasure of your company, I don't much care if I never see a mountain in my life. I have passed all my days in London, until I have formed as many and intense local attachments, as any of you mountaineers can have done with dead nature. The lighted shops of the Strand and Fleet Street, the innumerable trades, tradesmen and customers, coaches, waggons, playhouses, all the bustle and wickedness round about Covent Garden, the very women of the Town, the Watchmen, drunken scenes, rattles—life awake, if you awake, at all hours of the night, the impossibility of being dull in Fleet Street, the crowds, the very dirt and mud, the sun shining upon houses and pavements, the print shops, the old book stalls, parsons cheap'ning books, coffee houses, steams of soups from kitchens, the pantomimes, London itself a pantomime and a masquerade—all these things work themselves into my mind and feed me, without a power of satiating me.

And then later he adds: "My attachments are all local, pure local"; and calls his old rooms, his old chairs, the familiar streets and squares, his mistresses. His last years were saddened by his exile from London, at Enfield, and his complaints are not all humorous overstatements:

In dreams I am in Fleetmarket, but I wake and cry to sleep again. I die hard, a stubborn Eloisa in this detestable Paraclete. What have I gained by health?—intolerable dulness. What by early hours and moderate meals?—a total blank. O never let the lying poets be believed, who 'tice men from the cheerful haunts of streets—or think they mean it not of a country village. In the ruins of Palmyra I could gird myself up to solitude, or muse to the snorings of the Seven Sleepers, but to have a little teazing image of a town about one, country folk that do not look like country folks, shops two yards square, half a dozen apples and two penn'orth of overlooked gingerbread for the lofty fruiterers of Oxford Street, and, for the

immortal book and print stalls, a circulating
library that stands still. . . .

And there is all his intense humanism in the
concluding remarks of this paragraph:

> A garden was the primitive prison till man
> with promethean felicity and boldness luckily
> sinn'd himself out of it. Thence followed Babylon,
> Nineveh, Venice, London, haberdashers, gold-
> smiths, taverns, playhouses, satires, epigrams,
> puns—these all came in on the town part, and the
> thither side of innocence. Man found out
> inventions.

You can see his eyes dwelling fondly on them, a
little lighted heap of things in the great dark of this
life. He was attracted by the Quakers, but admits
that he could never endure their mystical quietude,
the white spaces in their universe:

> I am all over sophisticated, with humours,
> fancies, craving hourly sympathy. I must have
> books, pictures, theatres, chit-chat, scandal, jokes,
> ambiguities, and a thousand whim-whams, which
> their simpler taste can do without. I should
> starve at their primitive banquet. . . .

There is a genuine wistfulness in his whimsical
questioning of Death in the Essay on New Year's
Eves:

> Sun, and sky, and breeze, and solitary walks,
> and summer holidays, and the greenness of fields,

and the delicious juices of meats and fishes, and
society, and the cheerful glass, and candlelight,
and fireside conversations, and innocent vanities,
and jests, and *irony itself*—do these things go out
with life?

He lived so close to his friends, asked for and
gave so much sympathy, that the death of the least of
them takes something out of the world for ever:

> One sees a picture, reads an anecdote, starts
> a casual fancy, and thinks to tell of it to this
> person in preference to every other—the person is
> gone whom it would have peculiarly suited; it
> won't do for *another*. Every departure destroys
> a class of sympathies. There's Capt. Burney gone!
> what fun has whist now? What matters it what
> you lead, if you can no longer fancy him looking
> over you? . . . Thus one distributes oneself
> about—and now for so many parts of me I have
> lost the market. Common natures do not serve.
> Good people, as they are called, won't serve. I
> want individuals. I am made up of queer points
> and I want so many answering needles. . . .

Thus it is that he can give a peculiar poignancy to
any references he makes to a lost friend. When he
writes to Crabb Robinson, appealing for help from
the Benchers of the Inner Temple for the Norris
family, he communicates to every reader an aching
sense of loss:

> In him I have a loss the world cannot make up.
> He was my friend and my father's friend all the

life I can remember. I seem to have made foolish
friendships ever since. Those are friendships
which outlive a second generation. Old as I am
waxing, in his eyes I was still the child he first
knew me. To the last he called me Charley. I
have none to call me Charley now. . . .

These few sentences distil a larger measure of grief
and regret than the whole of Tennyson's *In
Memoriam*.

Nearly everything that Lamb ever wrote seems to
flower naturally out of his intimacies and affections.
Most of his essays have the tone of a meeting of old
friends. "Do you remember?" they cry to us; and
we find ourselves smiling and gulping. They are a
prose commentary on his poem on "the old familiar
faces." The thought of clerks from the vanished
South-Sea House, of the old Benchers of the Inner
Temple, leads him back to the Golden Age. They
were, it is true, "odd fishes"—it is his own phrase—
and nothing of their oddity is lost, but they are seen
in the lovely haze of affectionate reminiscence, they
are touched with a quaint poetry. This deep tide of
feeling is there all the time in Lamb. His wildest
pranks are only a delightful splash and glitter on its
surface. It goes flowing on through his oddest
letters. And because the roots in him are so strong
and fixed, he can afford to take pleasure in the mad
tangle of branches above, the blossoming of whim-
whams. About much of his humour there is a
suggestion of the happy family, the domestic joke.
He treats the *London Magazine* and its readers as if
they were a Christmas party. There is nothing public,

K

formal, solemn, impersonal about Lamb's authorship; it is all something done after hours; and
between friends, for fun; and in a country famous for
its amateurs, he is one of the greatest of amateur
authors.

He is for ever playing the madcap, but he does it
with a quaint gravity sufficient in itself to make him
unique. In his essays, his whimsies are sometimes a
thought too highly elaborated, but in his letters they
are perfect. His letters to Manning are full of them.
There is, for example, that one about Dick Hopkins,
"the swearing scullion of Caius"; and that wild
screed on Independent Tartary; and, best of all
perhaps, that long letter in which he rebukes
Manning, who was in China, for staying away so
long and then scatters death and desolation among
the people and places they both knew:

Empires have been overturned, crowns trodden
into dust, the face of the western world quite
changed: your friends have all got old—those you
left blooming—myself (who am one of the few
that remember you) those golden hairs which you
recollect my taking a pride in, turned to silver and
grey. Mary has been dead and buried many years,
she desired to be buried in the silk gown you sent
her. Rickman, that you remember, active and
strong, now walks out supported by a servant-
maid and a stick. Martin is a very old man. The
other day an aged woman knocked at my door,
and pretended to my acquaintance; it was long
before I had the most distant cognition of her;
but at last together we made her out to be Louisa,

the daughter of Mrs. Topham, formerly Mrs. Morton, who had been Mrs. Reynolds, formerly Mrs. Kenney, whose first husband was Holcroft, the dramatic writer of the last century. St. Paul's Church is a heap of ruins; the monument isn't half so high as you knew it, divers parts being successively taken down which the ravages of time had rendered dangerous; the horse at Charing Cross is gone, no one knows whither, and all this has taken place while you have been settling whether Ho-hing-tong should be spelt with a — or a —. For aught I see you had almost as well remain where you are, and not come like a Struldbug into a world where few were born when you went away. Scarce here and there one will be able to make out your face; all your opinions will be out of date, your jokes obsolete, your puns rejected with fastidiousness as wit of the last age. Your way of mathematics has already given way to a new method, which after all is, I believe, the old doctrine of Maclaurin, new-vamped up with what he borrowed of the negative quantity of fluxions from Euler.

Poor Godwin! I was passing his tomb the other day in Cripplegate churchyard. There are some verses upon it written by Miss Hayes, which if I thought good enough I would send you. He was one of those who would have hailed your return, not with boisterous shouts and clamours, but with the complacent gratulations of a philosopher anxious to promote knowledge as leading to happiness—but his systems and his theories are ten feet deep in Cripplegate mould. Coleridge is just dead, having lived just long enough to close the eyes of Wordsworth, who paid the debt to nature but a week or two before. Poor Col. but two days before he died wrote to a bookseller proposing an epic poem on the "Wanderings of Cain" in twenty-four books. It is said he has left behind him more than forty thousand treatises in criticism and metaphysics, but few of them in a state of completion. They are now destined, perhaps, to wrap up spices. . . . Gather up your wretched reliques, my friend, as fast as you can, and come to your old home. I will rub my eyes and try to recognise you. We will shake withered hands together, and talk of old things, of St. Mary's Church and the barber's opposite, where the young students in mathematics used to assemble. Poor Crisp, that kept it, afterwards set up a fruiterer's shop in Trumpington Street, and for aught I know, resides there still, for I saw the name up in the last journey I took there with my sister just before she died. I suppose you heard that I had left the India House, and gone into the Fishmongers' Almhouses over the bridge. I have a little cabin there, small and homely, but you shall be welcome to it. You like oysters, and to open them yourself; I'll get you some if you come in oyster time. . . .

There is a good deal that is characteristic of Lamb's humour in that letter; the wild inventions all gravely introduced, the shafts of critical wit here and there, the affectionate concern beneath the fooling, all these are characteristic.

There is no need, however, to begin quoting and illustrating and analysing in earnest. Except Shakespeare and Dickens, no humorist of ours—and how English Lamb is!—is better known; and even they are not better loved. There is something very odd about his fate. "Can a ghost laugh, or shake his gaunt sides?" he once asked. If it can, then his ghost must have shaken its gaunt sides many a time at the news from the solid world and daylight. The little things he scribbled between ledger and ledger, as it were, at the India House have long outlasted the epics of his friend Southey. The whimsical clerk has been promoted far above the solemn professional authors. And something better than this has happened, by a happy irony of fate. He was for ever troubled, as we have seen, by the mutability of things, the passing of old familiar faces, and much of what he wrote, half smiling and half in tears, is only a repetition in one form or another of his old cry: "All, all are gone." He saw everything he loved slipping away from him, the world growing stranger every day, and he wrote to keep it in front of him a little longer, to let others see it for a moment. But all the time he was bringing his own power of enchantment to things. His world is still alive, still smiles before us. The pipes and glasses and rubbers of whist and talks round the fire, he has preserved them all and has become the familiar companion of whole generations. A hundred years have passed and his fireside is not yet darkened, but warms a host of unknown friends.

CHAPTER VIII

DICKENS

FASHIONS come and fashions go, and now it is the French who are the greatest novelists in the world and now it is the Russians, but the supremacy of Dickens as a humorist remains unchallenged. We have only one name to put beside his, as a creator of humorous character, and that, of course, is Shakespeare. There is no comic figure in Dickens as great as Falstaff, who has in himself the very genius of humour. On the other hand, Shakespeare has not the same comic fecundity. Dickens is the creator of a whole population of drolls. There are nearly a hundred characters in *Pickwick* alone and nearly all of them are comic. He must have made more people laugh than the sum total of authors in several literatures. Like most things easy to enjoy, he is unusually difficult to criticize. We do not know where to begin. It is like being faced with a whole uproarious town: we can only point and shout.

The humour of Dickens is essentially a humour of character. It is his comic figures we remember first, before we remember the books that contain them. We all remember Mr. Peter Magnus, Mr. Sapsea, Mr. Guppy, Mr. Jack Hopkins, Mrs. Todgers, Mr. Toots, Mrs. Gamp, Mr. Pumblechook, Miss Nipper, but not all of us could allocate them to their several volumes without hesitation. Dickens lives chiefly now in his comic characters, but these are so numerous, so astonishing, so altogether delightful, that a writer could hardly wish for a better hold upon posterity. There was a time when people said these characters were great creations because we knew all about them, recognized them at a glance, and men went out about calling one another Pecksniffs and Mark Tapleys. It was then pointed out these were exactly the reasons why such characters were not great creations, that we knew so much about them precisely because they were not like human beings, that Pecksniff or Tapley merely meant hypocrisy and a gallant optimism. One side said that these characters were gross caricatures, and the other side said they were not. Both sides were right and both were wrong. The best of these characters are certainly great creations and they are equally certainly not like any human beings we have ever known. But to call them caricatures and have done is to arrive nowhere.

To those critics who have waved away these characters as easy and gross caricatures, we might apply the concluding words of Mrs. Sapsea's astonishing epitaph: "Stranger, pause. And ask thyself this question, Canst thou do likewise? If not, with a blush retire." Literature is full of caricatures, broad types, comic characters with a ruling passion, a single idea, an oft-repeated phrase, and for the simple reason that they are amusing and easy to do. But literature is not full of Dickens characters, and if anybody imagines that they are easy to do, let him try. Many of the adverse criticisms directed against Dickens simply miss him altogether to knock down some smaller and very different humorist, someone like Ben Jonson, who may be seen carefully putting together a few oddities. But what distinguishes Dickens is that there is in him a genuine creative force, a fountain of high spirits, a gushing spring of absurdity. People who refer one to his remarkable powers of observation and the like are misled and misleading; the secret lies in the quality of his imagination (which had something curiously childlike about it); there is in him a kind of poetry of the ludicrous. His best humour is not like real life but better than real life. It is significant that highly poetical people, such as Swinburne, have always delighted in the humour of Dickens; whereas stoutly prosaic persons, like Trollope, have never felt at home with it. It is larger than life.

The great Dickens drolls are not funny in the idea but in the actual expression of themselves. By this we mean that if they were merely described and not presented dramatically there would be little or nothing in them. This is not true of all comic characters. Thus it is not true of the Shandies or of some of Jane Austen's figures, such as Mr. Woodhouse. But the Dickens' characters are not there to be talked about but to talk, and it is in their sublimely idiotic talk that they and their creator achieve greatness. This may seem trivial or trite, yet it is by missing this point that many critics of Dickens have gone astray. Let us look at a few examples. There is Mr. Pecksniff. Now Mr. Pecksniff as a solid character, wedged into the plot, is of no importance at all, at least not now. He is not a solid character at all. Nor is the mere *idea* of him, that of a rascally ignorant architect who pretends to be unusually virtuous, a pattern of the moral order, either very credible or very amusing. We could all think of better characters than this ourselves. Pecksniff, then, is a rubbishy figure, mere hypocrisy with a tuft of hair. But no, he is nothing of the kind, because his actual talk on occasion is gloriously absurd. We could think of better characters than Pecksniff, but when it came to making them talk like this we should have to confess ourselves beaten and "with a blush retire." We have only to remember how Pecksniff improved the occasion in the coach to understand where the genius of Dickens makes its appearance:

"What are we?" said Mr. Pecksniff, "but coaches? Some of us are slow coaches——"

"Goodness, Pa!" cried Charity.

"Some of us, I say," resumed her parent with increased emphasis, "are slow coaches; some of us are fast coaches. Our passions are the horses; and rampant animals, too!"

"Really, Pa!" cried both the daughters at once. "How very unpleasant."

"And rampant animals, too!" repeated Mr. Pecksniff, with so much determination, that he may be said to have exhibited, at the moment, a sort of moral rampancy himself: "and Virtue is the drag. We start from The Mother's Arms, and we run to The Dust Shovel."

When he had said this, Mr. Pecksniff, being exhausted, took some further refreshment. When he had done that, he corked the bottle tight, with the air of a man who had effectually corked the subject also; and went to sleep for three stages.

What is important, then, about Mr. Pecksniff is not that he is a hypocritical architect who occasionally gets drunk, but that he can talk in this strain of sublime idiocy. If this is not like life, then, we say, so much the worse for life.

Again, Dick Swiveller is a type of character that is familiar enough in Victorian fiction. He is the young London clerk, with no money but plenty of high spirits. There are a good many such clerks in Trollope. But where Swiveller differs from the others (at least all those outside Dickens) is in the fact that, like Ancient Pistol, he is a creature compact of great phrases. Anybody might have *thought* of him, but only Dickens could have made him talk as he does, smacking his lips over his magnificently ridiculous phrases. It is not merely the fact that he can forget all his troubles in a friendly glass that is amusing, but the fact that when doing so he can call his glass of gin and cold water "the rosy wine" and can tell his friend (who is using the same tumbler) to "fan the sinking flame of hilarity with the wing of friendship," or that, after having been drunk the previous evening, he can cry:

What is the odds so long as the fire of soul is kindled at the taper of conviviality, and the wing of friendship never moults a feather!

Who but Dickens could have described the meeting of Dick and his friend, Mr. Chuckster, those two

Glorious Apollos? Or have contrived that Dick should lose his girl to a Mr. Cheggs, market-gardener?:

> "I came here," said Dick, rather oblivious of the purpose with which he had really come, "with my bosom expanded, my heart dilated, and my sentiments of a corresponding description. I go away with feelings that may be conceived, but cannot be described: feeling within myself the desolating truth that my best affections have experienced, this night, a stifler!"
>
> "I am sure I don't know what you mean, Mr. Swiveller," said Miss Sophy with downcast eyes. "I'm very sorry if——"
>
> "Sorry, ma'am!" said Dick, "sorry in the possession of a Cheggs! . . ."

How happy Dick (a man of phrases) is in his abyss of disillusion, radiating Byronic gloom!

Again, take Mrs. Gamp. She was, we are told, a satire upon what we might call the pre-Nightingale type of nurse, a drunken, grasping, ignorant, elderly woman, hardly fit to tend a sick dog. The deplorable habits of Mrs. Gamp were those, apparently, of a whole generation of so-called nurses, and Dickens' satirical portrait hastened the extinction of the type. But the actual conversation of Mrs. Gamp is a different matter altogether; it springs from Dickens' own wild genius of the absurd. As a talker, Mrs. Gamp is not a figure of satire but a creature from some fairy-tale of humour. Every word she utters is a joyful surprise. It would be worth being laid up only to listen to a nurse who could talk of "this Piljian's Projiss of a mortal wale," or ask for her pint of porter to be "brought reg'lar and draw'd mild." Such a creature could only have sprung out of a very furnace of humorous creation. Let us take another example from the dozens that offer themselves. There is Mrs. Todgers. The faded and anxious female who runs a shabby London boarding-house is a figure familiar enough in English fiction, but where do we find one that can talk of her troubles like Mrs. Todgers ?

"Presiding over an establishment like this, makes sad havoc with the features, my dear Miss Pecksniffs," said Mrs. Todgers. "The gravy alone, is enough to add twenty years to one's age, I do assure you.'

"Lor!" cried the two Miss Pecksniffs.

"The anxiety of that one item, my dears," said Mrs. Todgers, "keeps the mind continually upon the stretch. There is no such passion in human nature, as the passion for gravy among commercial gentlemen. It's nothing to say a joint won't yield —a whole animal wouldn't yield—the amount of gravy they expect each day at dinner. . . . You, my dears, having to deal with your pa's pupils who can't help themselves, are able to take your own way, but in a commercial establishment, where any gentleman may say, any Saturday evening: 'Mrs. Todgers, this day we part, in consequence of the cheese,' it is not so easy to preserve a pleasant understanding."

Mrs. Todgers may be a poor caterer but she is a superb phrase-maker.

Then, towering above them all, there is Mr. Micawber. You cannot dismiss Micawber by saying that he is an impecunious commercial traveller who is always waiting for something to turn up. There is a great deal more in him than that. But once more we can point out that it is not in the conception but in the actual execution of Micawber that Dickens displays his genius. It is what this glorious being actually says and does that is so incredibly rich. Nevertheless, he is a magnificently humorous conception. He is really the artist, the man of temperament, exiled among corn and coals. The secret of him is not— as is generally imagined—that he is a reckless optimist, but that he lives in a world of his own, where everything is larger and simpler and richer than in this world, where he himself, Wilkins Micawber, is the central figure of a colossal romance. His opulent and somewhat theatrical imagination has banished from this world of his all the drab shades, the grey little facts, the merely rational. Everything there is seen through a romantic haze and looms splendid or sinister, is dreadful in black or riotous in scarlet and gold. The most disastrous event only adds another chapter to the wonderful story that he sees unfolding before him. He really *enjoys* everything; the outside world, the real one, cannot get at him. If it sets the turncock from the waterworks upon him, he can talk about "the momentary laceration of a wounded spirit, made sensitive by a recent collision with the Minion of Power"; and a man who can refer to such an encounter in these terms, can see it as part of an epic, cannot be touched. The present, to him, is always a tremendous crisis, the latest scene in the drama, and, therefore, can be enjoyed; the past is an Othello's tale; and the future, already illuminating the next corner, is a happy ending. You will find that Mr. Micawber always talks about his affairs in this way. He is really an artist—of the large careless sort— and his work of art is his own life. He cannot be bothered with what we might call half-moods, will have no dull intervals, and so is always up or down. When David meets the two of them at Canterbury (they have been examining the Medway), they spend an uproariously happy evening together, putting away a huge dinner, brewing punch, drinking healths, and singing songs. Yet early the next morning, David receives that letter which begins:

My dear young Friend,
  The die is cast—all is over. Hiding the ravages of care with a sickly cast of mirth, I have not informed you, this evening, that there is no hope of the remittance! . . .

and signed by Mr. Micawber in the character of a "beggared outcast." David immediately rushes off to the hotel, hoping to comfort his wretched friends, but on the way sees the London coach with the two of them sitting up behind:

  Mr. Micawber, the very picture of tranquil enjoyment, smiling at Mrs. Micawber's conversation, eating walnuts out of a paper bag, with a bottle sticking out of his breast-pocket. . . .

Micawber had enjoyed being the beggared outcast just as much as he had enjoyed being the boon companion or the genial traveller.

The humour of Dickens has two sides, a satirical and a sympathetic. There were certain kinds of people he never tried to understand, stiff, cold, *official* sort of people, and these he turned into the victims of his satirical humour. As Clutton-Brock once remarked: "Everyone who fell into routine, who seemed to act inexpressively and with no sense of the fun of life, was turned by him into a marionette." His novels are full of such comic marionettes, masquerading as officials, lawyers, fashionable people, and bigwigs. His handling of them is frequently very funny—for Dickens was always determined to *enjoy* his characters, and even his most sinister villains are, as it were, a great lark, but they do not give us his best comic characters, which are the creations of his sympathetic humour. These, the Micawbers, the Wellers, Pickwick, Toots, and the rest, are always lovable simpletons, who ask for and receive the laughter of affection. There is something very queer about them, but it is not so much that they are caricatures, as people are so fond of saying, as that they are real people always seen from a certain angle. And from this angle they seem to be entirely compact of absurdity, so that they would still be funny, we feel, on their deathbeds, though, indeed, we cannot imagine one of them dying. We cannot imagine this because we do not think of these characters as being subject to the same fate as ourselves, as being inside Time, as sharing the common human lot of birth and death. We may love them

but we do not understand them. But it is not true
to say that we have never known people like them
or, alternatively, that we have never seen people
from this angle for ourselves. We have only to
return to our memories of our childhood to discover
that they are full of similar persons, potential Dickens'
characters. The odd adults we knew in those days,
the comic old friend of the family, a droll milkman
or butcher, reveal the outlines of Dickens' characters.
We saw these people as a queer, lovable assemblage
of tricks of voice and gesture; we never thought it
would be possible for them ever to be anything but
funny; and, however much we adored them, we
always saw them as creatures different from ourselves. This return to the childlike imagination is
the secret of both the great absurd Dickens' characters and his little marionettes. A Dickens' novel is
like the day and the night of some tremendous
excited child, now darkly miserable, now violently
happy. It is as if the little outcast he once was came
at last to set down on paper the daydreams he had
in the blacking factory, so that the cruel adults are
all severely punished, the cold sneering people are
turned into figures of fun dangling on the end of
wires and are mocked and buffeted, and all the
lovably comic souls are brought in and entertained
at a gigantic birthday-party. That is why the absurdities in Dickens can reach a poetical height, soar into
the blue: they are not a record of actuality but part
of a dream of life; they do not belong to things as
they are but to things as they ought to be.

It is impossible for us to say what made this
humour of his, to give its ingredients. We can only

notice his strong and curiously childlike imagination and his amazing energy and vitality. Leigh Hunt said of Dickens' face that "it has the life and soul in it of fifty human beings." This we can well believe when we read him. He put that life and soul into his books, in which the very *things*, the streets, houses, furniture, the very door-knockers, come to life, quiver with vitality. He would not have been the great humorist he is without that tremendous surge of life. Nor would he, perhaps, have been a humorist at all if he had not also had that extreme sensibility which makes him quicken to any warmth of heart. With his very clear and simple outlook upon men and affairs, his militant temper, his great energy, he might simply have been one of the most forceful and perhaps one of the crudest of our satirists. But he was always swept forward on a wave of sympathy and pity. He was a waif who suddenly found himself in possession of a magic wand, and, remembering his own life in the dark streets, waved that wand so that everybody might share, with laughter and tears, the life of vast multitudes of the poor and simple. Humour in him can be compared to the lyrical passion of the poet. Even its history is not dissimilar. No poet can maintain that first careless rapture; the lyrical flow does not come so easily as the years pass; until at last it stops altogether or only gushes out occasionally when he is unusually deeply moved. So it is with Dickens' humour. His art progressed as he grew older; the later Dickens is a novelist and not simply an astonishing improvisator; but the enchanting high spirits, the riot of absurdity of his earlier work, is not to be found in the later. By the

L

time he had taken to keeping notebooks and working up his fun methodically, the rot had fairly set in. Long before the notebooks appeared, however, as far back as *Dombey and Son*, we feel that the humorist has lost something of his spring. It is true that *Dombey and Son* can show us Mr. Toots and Susan Nipper, fresh genuine creations of humour, but it shows us, too, those eccentric wooden figures that merely repeat certain catchwords and gestures, figures that appear increasingly later. *David Copperfield*, we admit, gives us the old soaring spirit of fun: there is all of Dickens in this, his masterpiece. But then there is a falling off of humour in *Bleak House*, a collapse of it in *Hard Times*, and nothing like a real recovery in *Little Dorrit* and *Great Expectations*. Many people, including critics of note, tell us that he recaptured the old spirit in *Our Mutual Friend*, that Silas Wegg and Boffin and the rest are the equals of the Wellers, the Crummleses, the Micawbers, and other earlier creations; but they have never succeeded in convincing us, in blinding us to the fact that, amusing as they are, there is something forced and mechanical about the Weggs and Boffins. There is, of course, many a gush of that genuine humour of his in the later novels, but the spring itself, splashing down the roads of England in *Pickwick* and *Nicholas Nickleby* and flooding America itself in *Martin Chuzzlewit*, is no longer foaming there. But what a torrent it is! How it has brightened the world with its pity and innocent laughter!

CHAPTER IX

SHAKESPEARE

SHAKESPEARE has long been the world's pride, yet he drew his breath as an Englishman and he remains English. The Germans may turn him into a nest of philosophical problems; the French may turn him into so much sonorous stage rhetoric; the Italians may turn him into tearing passion and grand opera; the Americans—most whimsical of all—may turn him into Bacon; all these may lay hold of him and translate him even as Bottom was translated; but he remains English. We, who walk where he walked, have been often accused of neglecting our greatest genius; we do not, it seems, write enough long, solemn books about him or set him on the stage often enough. This may be true, though it overlooks the fact that we began about a hundred and fifty years earlier than other nations, that all our literary dictators, from Ben Jonson to Coleridge, said their say of him, that all our greatest actors and actresses have always made their reputations in his parts. Yet it misses the mark: it is as if were told we did not enjoy the spring flowers because they were not mentioned in the papers, because no notice about them is posted in the clubs. These distant critics forget that we have grown up with Shakespeare, that we have, indeed, breathed his very air. This is unfortunate in some respects.

Thus it prevents our suddenly discovering him: the man who went to see *Hamlet* and complained that it was all quotations was an Englishman. Our gains, however, have been colossal. England and Shakespeare are inextricably intertwined; strands of his weaving run through the fabric of our national thought, literature, life. And there are two out of the many gigantic legacies he left the world that we in England are peculiarly fitted to enjoy. The first is his poetry, the actual dance and glitter of verse. Ths second is his humour, which is our present concern.

We never feel that there is anything local and particular about Shakespeare's Tragedy. He goes far afield, out of his own time, away from his own places, for its scenes, to mediæval Denmark, to a mythical Ancient Britain, to Venice, to Roman Egypt, but the spirit of it travels further still, out of time and place. Wherever the evil webs are spun and the noble and generous heart is caught for a season, there are the frosted battlements of Elsinore and the thunder and lightning of *Lear*. Any overmastering passion builds again the palaces of Cleopatra; and every affrighted conscience see Birnam forest come to Dunsinane. But, indeed, these tragedies—in Raleigh's fine words—" deal with greater things than man; with powers and passions, elemental forces, and dark abysses of suffering; with the central fire, which breaks through the thin crust of civilization, and makes a splendour in the sky above the blackness of ruined homes." Small wonder then that they should reach out to universality. Once they have conquered, with dark thundering armies, our imagination, we never think of allotting to him who wrote them a nationality, a period: a man came who had, for a season, dreadful visions of our life in this place, and made out of such visions these masterpieces; that is all. But when we turn to his Comedy, at once we grasp the local and particular. The scenes take us far afield again, to Athens and Illyria and maritime Bohemia, but this time the spirit of it does not travel further but remains obstinately at home, where humour, like charity, begins. Hamlet and Othello and Antony may be good, bad, or indifferent Danes, Moors, Romans; it does not matter; either they could come from nowhere or they could come from anywhere; but Bottom and his friends have obviously not been fetched from ancient Athens, for they are as English as the beer with which they most certainly regaled themselves after their famous performance. Duke Orsino and Viola and Olivia—not tragic nor yet quite comic characters—could very well come from Illyria or any other place this side of Asia, but when we consider Sir Toby Belch and his friend, Sir Andrew Aguecheek, we can only conclude that Illyria must be very near these shores: there is an English smack about both the rogue and the butt. Shakespeare's Messina is filled with Leonatos and Claudios and Don Pedros, fashioning the courtly intrigue, but the fellows who keep the watch and contrive the low comedy are called Dogberry and Hugh Oatcake and George Seacoal, and, in truth, have clearly never been more than two miles away from an English alehouse. Lastly, at his highest pitch of humour, Shakespeare makes not even a pretence of leaving these shores. The figure of Falstaff is revealed against a background of London City and the Cotswold Hills.

In his comedies, Shakespeare is a poetic humorist rather than a creator of Comedy proper. Malvolio is perhaps the best example of a character that Shakespeare handles in the traditional manner of the creator of Comedy. Malvolio is not a fool treated with indulgence, given leave to exhibit his folly at length, but is a serious character hunted down with contemptuous laughter. He represents a type that Shakespeare disliked, a cold and conceited fellow, sick with self-love and rotten with envy, and had the play that contains him been of a tragic cast, we might have seen Malvolio playing a very different part, one nearer that of Iago. As it is a comedy, he is laughed at, but the laughter is not the usual affectionate outburst but is keen and cutting. Sir Andrew is really a more contemptible figure than the capable steward, yet he is simply enjoyed and not derided. Shakespeare only asks us to enjoy him and not to criticize him. But when he comes to Malvolio, Shakespeare for once makes himself the guardian of society and good sense, and gives the man a flick or two of the lash. But Malvolio—a typical figure of Comedy proper—has always been regarded as an odd and puzzling character, standing quite apart from the majority of Shakespeare's comic figures.

These comedies have a special atmosphere of their own; their characters are seen through a lovely poetic haze. The lovers in *A Midsummer Night's Dream*, Rosalind and her Orlando, Viola and Olivia and the Duke and Sebastian, even Benedick and Beatrice, all these figures fence wittily and exchange the glittering passes of Comedy, but they are not seen in the dry light of the purely intellectual comic writer, and are not to be hunted down in the interests of good sense and the best usages of society. Their world—as Raleigh remarked—"is a rainbow world of love in idleness. The intensities and realities of life shimmer into smoke and film in that delicate air." Each comedy seems to have its own delightful atmosphere: *A Midsummer Night's Dream* is all moonshine and gossamer threads; *As You Like It* is a daydream in a forest glade, full of golden light and green distances; *Twelfth Night* is one of those delightful Tudor gardens turned into a play, the biggest tulip calling herself Olivia. It is impossible for us to think of these plays as so much character and event, a mere elaborate tracing in black-and-white, for they remain in our imagination full of changing light and colour; they are a bewilderment of sweet airs; like the lover, they have eyes of youth, they speak holiday, they smell April and May. When we consider these comedies we find ourselves faced with Shakespeare the poet. His humour, it is true, is everywhere, even the grimmest and wildest tragedies cannot keep it out; but if we are to look at it more closely, we must restrict ourselves to the broadly comic scenes and characters.

Once the tragic fit has passed, once the smoking depths and star-crowned heights have vanished, the breadth of Shakespeare's imagination dowered him with a tolerance of his fellow creatures, an easy sympathy with whatever manner of man came before him, that have never been surpassed. If he goes in search of folly, it is not to hoot it out of the world, but to enjoy it. He indulges his fools, gently dandles their innocent imbecilities before our eyes, yet seems to allow Nature herself—no matter how small and silly her voice—to speak through them. To those who would point the finger of scorn at the ragged and idiotic company he can sometimes empty upon his stage, we can imagine him retorting as Falstaff retorted to Prince Hal's comment upon his pitiful rascals: "Tush, man, mortal men, mortal men." These oddities have their place with the rest of us on this earth—they are born, see the sun, have their little say, and die, and we cannot refuse to entertain them. Consider Feeble, the woman's tailor, who only appears for a few minutes among the grotesque recruits in Shallow's orchard, a creature seemingly of no more importance than a yard or two of his tape and thread, a mere shadow of a poor fellow. Yet what an answer he makes to Bardolph when he sees he must go:

> By my troth, I care not; a man can die but once; we owe God a death: I'll ne'er bear a base mind: an't be my destiny, so; an't be not, so: no man's too good to serve's prince; and, let it go which way it will, he that dies this year is quit for the next.

It is as if a wandering light suddenly fixed itself on his face and figure, clearly revealing every feature and fumbling gesture, as if his little trembling voice—naked humanity itself speaking out of its bewilderment—were at our very ears. There is the same genius in that tiny speech that fashioned the miraculous utterances of the great tragic characters. Francis Feeble, woman's tailor of Gloucestershire, is there for ever.

Into the most attenuated grotesques, the dimmest rural shades, Shakespeare can breathe life, so that they speak in their own voices though it be only in the tiniest whisper. In the far spaces of that solar system of which Sir John himself is the great round roaring sun may be found that shrunken cinder of a planet, Justice Shallow. Yet this poor thing, moving in the dark outer spaces, has its own satellites, Silence and Slender, those faint little moons. The lives of both these creatures can flower in the watery sunshine of their great cousin, the Justice. And though both of them are—as Hazlitt says—shadows of shades, tottering on the brink of nothing, yet they are by no means exactly alike; they have their individual differences. Silence is old silliness, and Slender is young silliness: one seems to speak in a husky whisper, the other in a piping treble. Only Slender could have had that scene with Anne Page:

> *Anne*—Will't please your Worship to come in, sir?
>
> *Slender*—No, I thank you, forsooth, heartily; I am very well.
>
> *Anne*—The dinner attends you, sir.
>
> *Slender*—I am not a-hungry, I thank you; forsooth. Go, sirrah, for all you are my man, go wait upon my cousin Shallow. (*Exit Simple.*) A justice of peace sometime may be beholden to his friend for a man. I keep but three men and a

boy yet, till my mother be dead: but what though? yet I live like a poor gentleman born.

Anne—I may not go in without your Worship: they will not sit till you come.

Slender—I'faith, I'll eat nothing; I thank you as much as though I did.

Anne—I pray you, sir, walk in.

Slender—I had rather walk here, I thank you. I bruised my shin th'other day with playing at sword and dagger with a master of fence, three veneys for a dish of stew'd prunes; and, by my troth, I cannot abide the smell of hot meat since. Why do your dogs bark so? be there bears i' the town?

Anne—I think there are, sir; I heard them talk'd of.

Slender—I love the sport well; but I shall as soon quarrel at it as any man in England. You are afraid, if you see the bear loose, are you not?

Anne—Ay, indeed, sir.

Slender—That's meat and drink to me, now. I have seen Sackerson loose twenty times, and have taken him by the chain; but, I warrant you, the women have so cried and shriek'd at it, that it pass'd: but women, indeed, cannot abide 'em; they are very ill-favour'd rough things."

We can fairly see his innocent vacuous face, his pink cheeks and little yellow beard. Silence is older and much humbler; he is happy prompting his cousin Shallow to disclose his greatness and his wild youth; he only asks to sit in the orchard, over the carraways and pippins, while the great men talk together. Yet the wine stirs in him as it does in the others; he can break unbidden into song, lifting his voice like some roistering sparrow; he can answer Falstaff's ironic remark by declaring he has "been merry twice and once ere now," thus flashing a light upon a little desert of a life; he can even answer the tremendous Pistol, who says that Falstaff is now one of the greatest men in the realm, by agreeing but at the same time indicating the claims of some obscure rural hero of his: "By'r Lady, I think 'a be, but Goodman Puff of Barson." What a miraculous talk is that he has with Shallow when we first meet them in the play! Silence, so proud of being where he is, so foolish and simple; Shallow, so fussy, vain and prattling, never able to keep to the point for two sentences together and never forgetting his own importance:

Shallow The same Sir John, the very same. I saw him break Skogan's head at the court-gate, when 'a was a crack not thus high: and the very same day did I fight with one Sampson Stockfish, a fruiterer, behind Gray's Inn. Jesu, Jesu, the mad days that I have spent! and to see how many of my old acquaintance are dead!

Silence—We shall all follow, cousin.

Shallow—Certain, 'tis certain; very sure, very sure: death, as the Psalmist saith, is certain to all; all shall die. How a good yoke of bullocks at Stamford Fair?

Silence—Truly, cousin, I was not there.

Shallow—Death is certain. Is old Double of your town living yet?

Silence—Dead, sir.

Shallow—Jesu, Jesu, dead! 'a drew a good bow; and dead! 'a shot a fine shoot: John o' Gaunt loved him well, and betted much money on his head. Dead! 'a would have clapped i' the clout at twelve score; and carried you a forehand shaft a fourteen and fourteen and a half, that it would have done a man's heart good to see. How a score of ewes now?

Silence—Thereafter as they be: a score of good ewes may be worth ten pounds.

Shallow: And is old Double dead?

This is humour that goes down to the very roots of this life; it is laughter lit with wonder.

Sir Andrew Aguecheek is another country booby, cousin to these Gloucestershire folk for all that his address is Illyria; yet he, too, has a character of his own. He has no brains, no will, no courage, neither self-confidence nor self-respect; only a little wealth and a great deal of folly; but the all-too-obvious ebb and flow of his conceit, his lack of guile, his childlike capacity for wonder and pleasure, these are delightful. His poor mind is as open to the sight as the face of the town clock. How delicious is his answer, when Sir Toby accuses him of being "put down!" "Methinks sometimes I have no more wit than a Christian or an ordinary man has: but I am a great eater of beef, and I believe that does harm to my wit." And his reply when Sir Toby asks if our life does not consist of the four elements: "Faith, so they say; but I think it rather consists of eating and drinking." When the Clown asks if they will have a love-song or a song of good life, Sir Toby decides

for the former, and Sir Andrew hastens to agree:
"Ay, ay: I care not for good life." What could be
better than his critical observation on the matter of
Sir Toby's fooling: "Ay, he does well enough if he
be disposed, and so do I too; he does it with a better
grace, but I do it more natural." When he is told
that Malvolio is a kind of Puritan, he cries: "O! if I
thought that, I'd beat him like a dog," though when
pressed for his reason, he admits to having none:
he merely wishes to stand well with the company.
When Sir Toby says that he is adored by Maria, Sir
Andrew will not be left behind and declares, with
almost pathetic naïveté: "I was adored once";
though nobody believes him. When he overhears
some mention of "a foolish knight," he has no doubt
who the person is: "That's me, I warrant you"; and
when, the moment after, he actually hears his name,
he is positively triumphant: "I knew 'twas I, for
many do call me fool." He does not mind, for he
would rather be mentioned, singled out, even as a
fool than passed without notice altogether. To the
last he keeps his faith in his boon companion and
hero, Sir Toby, and when they have got broken
heads and "bloody coxcombs" for their pains at the
end, he can say: "I'll help you, Sir Toby, because
we'll be dressed together." We feel sorry for the
poor simpleton when Sir Toby turns and abuses him.
Let us hope they made their peace together afterwards.

Different again from any of these are Bottom and
his friends. The play they figure in is earlier and was
written in a different mood. The humour of Bottom
and Peter Quince has not the same depth as that of

Shallow and Silence. The Athenian artisans (directly imported from rural England) are figures of fun rather than humorous characters, though Bottom himself perhaps is an exception. He is the most substantial character in the whole mad piece, as solid as a hill, and the first of Shakespeare's immortal drolls. We see him against a moonlit gossamer background of elves and fays and so he appears the most prosaic of weavers, but if we study him in his own world, we shall see that he is really a romantic, the only one of his company fit to be called to such a destiny. He has, in his own way, the soaring imagination (and conceit) of the artist: that is why he is ready to play any and every part, lover and tyrant, lady and lion; he, too, is a child of vanity and vision. He *sees* himself in every part: "That will ask some tears in the true performing of it: if I do it, let the audience look to their eyes; I will move storms, I will condole in some measure"; the lion's part is nothing but roaring, but Bottom jumps at it and is willing to promise either a very full-blooded performance, which will please the Duke, or a delicately modulated roar for the ladies. He is at once eager and yet discriminating in the matter of beards, his choice and fancy ranging from your straw-colour to your purple-in-grain. He is the only one of the players who wants to make a success of the piece for its own sake. Among the fairies, he proves himself to be a much better man than the wretched imitation Falstaff of *The Merry Wives of Windsor*. When the lovely Titania confesses at once that she is enamoured of him, he carries off the situation in a brave masculine fashion, like a true humorist, man of the world, and philospher: "Methinks, mistress, you should have little reason for that: and yet, to say the truth, reason and love keep little company together nowadays; the more the pity that some honest neighbours will not make them friends. Nay, I can gleek upon occasion." His remark about reason and love might be taken as the motto of the play. He is humorous and condescending with his strange little servitors, like a typical English sailor in Japan:

> Monsieur Cobweb, good monsieur, get your weapons in your hand, and kill me a red-hipp'd humble-bee on the top of a thistle; and, good monsieur, bring me the honey-bag. Do not fret yourself too much in the action, monsieur; and, good monsieur, have a care the honey-bag break not. I would be loth to have you overflown with a honey-bag, signior.

He can make himself at home anywhere, even in Elfland. It is doubtful if he does not enjoy his ass's head, for about many of his remarks: "I could munch your good dry oats. Methinks I have a great desire to a pottle of hay: good hay, sweet hay, hath no fellow," there is a certain consciously humorous smack. Yet when he awakes to his own world again, the wonder of it all breaks out in him:

> I have had a most rare vision. I have had a dream, past the wit of man to say what dream it was: man is but an ass, if he go about to expound this dream. . . . The eye of man hath not heard, the ear of man hath not seen, man's hand is not

able to taste, his tongue to conceive, nor his heart
to report, what my dream was. . . .

But away he rushes to take command of the play-
acting. He was never in ancient Athens, but he has
been here in England—a large, round-faced fellow,
oracular over pots of beer—these many hundreds of
years. You can go into rural tap-rooms and find him,
and after enjoying his company for an hour, you will
come to wonder if he has been laughing at you just
as you have been laughing at him. Shakespeare knew
him well, and only he could have thought of luring
him into the heart of Faerie.

At the other extreme from these simpletons are
the conscious wits. Among these are the clowns, the
professional humorists. The most famous of them is,
perhaps, Touchstone, whose bright motley stands out
in such relief in the Forest of Arden. We cannot really
laugh *at* him because even when he becomes a butt
he has deliberately turned himself into one, is indeed
only angling for our laughter. Some of his fun—and
this applies even more to most of his fellow clowns—
does not amuse very much now because it consists
in verbal quibbling, a game of battledore with the
dictionary as shuttlecock. But at its best it is a
critical humour. The Duke understood Touchstone
when he remarked: "He uses his folly like a stalking-
horse, and, under the presentation of that, he shoots
his wit." His method of criticism is chiefly by way of
parody; he plays courtier, lover, and pastoral philosopher, like the rest, but contrives that everything he
does shall be exaggerated and absurd. He is the
ambassador, in this realm of idealization, of the

comic spirit. His mockery implies that reality is still going on somewhere and that it is very different from what passes in Arden. Courtship and marriage, the pastoral life, codes of honour, all these are passed before his humorous gaze, his ripe disillusionment. Perhaps the wisest things said in this Forest come from the Fool.

Sir Toby Belch is a coarse, swashbuckling old rip, but he is a wit rather than a simpleton. We discover his philosophy in his opening remark: "Care's an enemy to life." We see him spend the rest of his time driving away care with floods of sack, showers of pickled herrings, songs and catches and happy hours of fool-baiting. He has the air of one for ever half-seas-over but never quite at a loss for a witty rejoinder. There is a gusto in his mischief-making that is delightful. He runs between the disguised Viola and Sir Andrew, when the terrified pair would be duelling, in an ecstasy of pleasure, now raising their courage and now damping it. It is impossible not to like the mischievous old toper. His most famous remark is, of course, the one he made when he was rebuked by Malvolio; and though the Malvolios have since multiplied beyond computation and have crept into larger offices than that of steward, they have not yet succeeded in finding a suitable retort to Sir Toby when he cries: "Dost thou think, because thou art virtuous, there shall be no more cakes and ale?"

But an infinitely greater character follows close upon Sir Toby's heels and overshadows him. It is late in the day either to describe or praise that comic genius, not only witty in himself, but the cause that

wit is in other men, Sir John Falstaff. He was
brought in to be one character out of a great many in
two historical plays, but he grew at once to such a
stature that history itself is but a back-cloth for him.
Raleigh puts it well when he says:

> He bestrides the play like a Colossus, and the
> young gallants walk under his huge legs and peep
> about to find themselves honourable graves. In
> all stress of circumstance, hunted by misfortune
> and disgrace, he rises to the occasion, so that the
> play takes on the colour of the popular beast-fable;
> our chief concern is that the hero shall never be
> outwitted; and he never is.

Humour in literature has never reached a higher
strain than it does in this astounding character, to
whom every device by which laughter can be raised
is familiar, who makes himself his own butt for our
delight and yet remains invulnerable. His followers
and companions are not to be despised. Bardolph
is mostly nose, and Nym mostly "humours"; but
Ancient Pistol is an astonishing grotesque, a walking
parody of highfalutin, a comic figure made out of
paper and ink, who can in a single one of his innumerable daft phrases, such as "Under which king,
Besonian? speak or die?" sum up a whole school of
bad literature, but who yet contrives to be a real
person. How excellent too are Hostess Quickly, who
for ever wavers between a love of mirth and easy
living and a desire to be thought respectable, to have
a good name in the parish; and her companion, Doll
Tearsheet, with her pretended delicacy and loud

railing tongue, her one supremely natural touch of sentiment: "Come, I'll be friends with thee, Jack: thou art going to the wars; and whether I shall ever see thee again or no, there is nobody cares." But towering above them all is the glorious fat knight, a mountain of good-fellowship, a cascade of wit and droll imagery, who can lay traps for everybody's good humour, even turning an angry Chief Justice into a laughing fellow wit. "Would I were with him, wheresome'er he is, either in Heaven or in Hell!" cries poor Bardolph, his butt for thirty years, when he hears of his master's death. We feel that Hell itself could not subdue that spirit of his, that the place would crumble at his touch. He stands four-square in the centre of a comic vision of this life, and after three centuries he still looks in vain for an equal to stand beside him. It was said of him that he larded the lean earth as he walked along, and we who love him are ready to take the sneer and transform it into a glorious epitaph.

What a world of wit and high spirits and happy laughter is here! face after face, scene after scene, enchantingly etched, return to the memory: the gay Mercutio and the prattling Nurse; Bottom and Peter Quince in the magic wood; Rosalind and Touchstone capping jests; Sir Toby, Sir Andrew, and the clown at their catches; Benedick and Beatrice playing lovers, and Dogberry addressing the Watch; Slender and Sir Hugh Evans at Windsor; Pistol and Fluellen at the wars; Autolycus cozening the Shepherds; Falstaff marching his ragged regiment into immortality: to think of this world is to stand beside Prospero and watch him point his wand. The master of the revels, smiling so serenely at his enchanting shadows, lived here and breathed this air. Of the width and splendour of imagination to be found in this whole world of humour that Shakespeare created, it is not necessary to speak; we could not copy it if we tried; we can only wonder and give praise. There is, however, in this world of his an air of large tolerance, of superb magnanimity, that is ours for the asking. We like to think good nature, tolerance, kindness are English qualities, and certainly they are necessary for humour, of which we have never had any lack. Shakespeare, who "takes up the meanest subjects with the same tenderness that we do an insect's wing, and would not kill a fly," does but head and crown the list of our humorists, men who have not lent their wits to an inquisition but have laughed out of the depths of their affections: "Mortal men, mortal men!" cries Falstaff; and then, long after, in the sunset close of *Cymbeline*, comes "Pardon's the word for all." It would be better for us to be once more a small out-landish people and yet be renowned for this spirit than to bestride the earth and lose our laughter in gloom, suspicion, and hate. Shakespeare and Dickens and all their fellow humorists were once here, and we must not fail them. Just as our humour is one of our most glorious heritages, so, too, it is not the least of our trusts.

PRINTED IN GREAT BRITAIN BY J. AND J. GRAY, EDINBURGH